FRIDAY'S CHILD

# Friday's Child

## Sandra Crossley

Mandarin Press

Copyright © Sandra Crossley 2004
First published in 2004 by Mandarin Press
Loundshay Manor Cottage, Preston Bowyer, Milverton
Somerset TA4 1QF
website: www.amolibros.com
tel/fax 01823 401527

Reprinted 2006

Distributed by Gazelle Book Services Limited
Hightown, White Cross Mills, South Rd, Lancaster
England LA1 4XS

The right of Sandra Crossley to be identified as the author of the work has been asserted herein in accordance with the Copyright, Designs and Patents Act 1988.

All rights reserved. This book is sold subject to the condition that it shall not, by way of trade or otherwise, be lent, resold, hired out or otherwise circulated without the publisher's prior consent in any form of binding or cover other than that in which it is published and without a similar condition including this condition being imposed on the subsequent purchaser.

British Library Cataloguing in Publication Data
A catalogue record for this book is available from the British Library.

ISBN 0-9545834-0-X
ISBN 978-0-9545834-0-8

Typeset by Amolibros, Milverton, Somerset
This book production has been managed by Amolibros
Printed and bound by T J International Ltd, Padstow, Cornwall, UK

# Acknowledgements

To my children and grandchildren, 'my family'.

To my soulmate, Jon, Jacky, a special friend, and to Ian for empowering me to do this. To Callum, for being Callum…

And to the memory of Louise, my mum. Were it not for her cocooning me in the security and love she gave in those early years, and which sustained me in my darkest days, I am sure I would not have had the strength to endure, and be writing this today.

# PRELUDE

My head is bursting, blood is trickling from my nose, my knees are knocking as I try to regain control of my body; I'm holding on to the door frame for support as I clamber upwards, terrified that the whole performance is going to be repeated again, hardly daring to breathe for fear of drawing attention to myself. And for the first time I question why?

It is my thirteenth birthday and, childlike, in a moment of euphoria and excitement reminiscent of the old days when special occasions were a matter of celebration, of love and surprises, I quite simply in that split second 'forget' and ask if there are any birthday cards or presents for me.

Regretting the words even before I finish saying them and with that sinking feeling in my stomach that I have come to experience so often, knowing that repercussions are on their way, I watch as my stepmother turns towards me, almost in slow motion. I brace myself for the onslaught, praying that I will be strong enough to withstand it.

*I am greeted with a tirade of abuse, that I am an ungrateful, grasping creature, that I am lucky enough to be given a roof over my head when I'm not even a part of their family...that I don't 'belong'.*

*Building in ferocity as my stepmother loses her control, inevitably the beating starts as I had known it would; the only thought in my head at this moment is to survive, and as always, I wonder if this day is going to be my last.*

*Quivering in the aftermath, every orifice of my frail body on fire, I again ask myself: why? Where did it all begin? What have I done that is so terrible?*

*Happy Birthday, Friday's Child!*

# —ONE—
# GOODBYES

**B**eing adopted meant no more to me than the knowledge that I was 'an extra-special, chosen child', cocooned in a web of utter love and devotion. Occasionally I wondered why my father, whenever he introduced me to anyone, always prefixed it by saying, 'This is my special, chosen, adopted daughter Sandra,' (rather as if he were choosing his favourite centre from a box of chocolates!) but it didn't worry me unduly. Dad said it was because he wanted everyone to know how lucky he was. I loved him but he didn't feature overly in my life. It was my mum who was 'my world', for whom I was 'truly special and chosen'. The amount of love she lavished on me left me in no doubt that I was indeed a very cherished, lucky little girl.

I had a wonderful childhood marred only by the fact that Mum was always ill and away in hospital somewhere or another, usually University College in London. My formative years were thus moulded in the bosom of Mum's large and caring family of brothers and sisters. They seemed to take it in turns to envelop me into the heart of their families when Louise (Mum) was out of action. I loved them dearly.

Dad was mostly around too, when he wasn't at work. He was loving towards me, always caring and tender towards Louise, solicitous to her needs being so poorly, and I can never remember anything but warmth and love flowing between them.

I was a happy, sunny child with a permanent smile on my face and, as with most children, without a care in the world really. I took totally for granted the love and attention that was always there for me.

Because of Louise's recurring illness, most of my school holidays were spent with big bouncy Uncle Fred, my mother's eldest brother, his wife Chris and their three offspring, all slightly older than me, doing all the things that Enid Blyton's *Secret Five* books were made of. There was a menagerie of animals, ponies and a sprawling house. It was an idyllic lifestyle, particularly for an only child like me, to be a part of the rivalry and camaraderie of other children.

When Louise was in hospital, which was much of the time really, I was 'shared' during the school term between Auntie Ciss and Nell, Mum's eldest sisters, both spinsters who had remained in the house where my grandparents had lived and their parents before them. Auntie Ciss was quite dizzy, with big rosy cheeks, a stutter which endeared you even more to her, and a life full of fun, whilst Nell was austere and very sensible, always telling Auntie Ciss off, a person to have a very healthy respect for. But both had in common that they loved and cherished me to death.

Next door lived Uncle George with his stutter and lame leg, a victim of Parkinson's Disease which caused him a lot of pain. He always had a smile on his face for me, a broad knee for a cuddle and a bar of chocolate or a treat for me which he'd produce from behind his back, making me guess which hand it was hidden in. Next door to him lived my Auntie Gwen and Uncle Bert who also had an adopted daughter, though grown-up, and living with her family just across the road. Always looking out for each other, 'my' family were what would generally be termed 'the salt of the earth'. There wasn't a lot of money between them, but Auntie Gwen was always popping back from a shopping trip with a remnant of material to make into a dress or something or other for me.

Uncle Bert worked for the council; as a cleaner; he used to come home covered from head to foot in dust, his wrinkly face sweat-lined and weary. My Auntie Gwen always used to shout at him to take his dirty clothes off but he used to ignore her, winking at me behind her back and flopping down in his comfy armchair. A cloud of dust would fill the room and five minutes later he'd be fast asleep. Saturdays was his rest day, his treat as he called it. He'd sit and listen to the sport on the radio and at tea time he'd have a huge dish of winkles and cockles which my auntie had fetched for him that morning. I thought they were awful although I used to be mesmerised by his carefully extracting them with his pin. He was full of mischief, he'd say, 'Eek, this one's all wet and slimy, have a taste, me lovely,' and chase me round the room, both of us laughing fit to burst and the winkle more often than not landing up on Auntie Gwen's clean floor, much to her disgust. I loved my Uncle Bert.

Just further down the road lived my Uncle Jack and Auntie Marian; they too had three daughters and always gave me the warmest of welcomes. There were other welcoming aunts and uncles living in the vicinity too, and, collectively, they all played an enormous part in ensuring my life was full of stability and love whilst Louise was away.

Living totally unpretentiously in little back-to-back houses next door to each other in Ealing, I flitted back and forwards from them all in happy harmony—just a normal common-or-garden family I guess to most people but they were lifelines to me.

Louise was the baby of this large family, much adored by them all, probably because a more gentle, caring person you couldn't wish to meet.

I think each and every one of them would have taken her pain onto their own shoulders, if they could have done so, to spare her; and taking on the care of me, 'her reason for living' as she would always call me, was something they did unstintingly.

I was a lucky, very loved little girl.

Louise occasionally, when fleetingly her disease went into remission, came home and on those occasions I moved back to live at home. I can never remember her being anything but perfection. This was a special, gentle, lady, always smiling, in spite of being wracked with pain, and I did my best, in the inimitable style of a child, to help with her care. I absolutely adored her and she in turn cocooned me in so much warmth and love that it was more than enough to sustain me through the times I couldn't share my life with her.

Dad was around at these times, caring, but always

immersed in work. I suppose one would call him a professional man, a white-collar worker. Hindsight would show me now that work became his therapy for his inability to help Louise who was apparently full of cancer. An articulate, scholarly man, he was tender and loving around her but the inadequacy that he obviously felt in his failure to take away the ravages that this all-consuming, dreadful disease invokes, in having to stand helpless on the sidelines watching her suffer, were just, for much of the time, too much to bear. He would find excuses, any excuses, relating to the rigours of work, to absent himself rather than face the harsh realities.

Our house was always full of love and laughter, though; Louise's family were always there to share the care, for every day that she remained with us they considered a gift of God; and, given the circumstances, it was.

Diagnosed with breast cancer when I was a few months old, she wasn't expected to make my first birthday, but I was her world, her reason for living and by some miracle she stayed with me, lighting my life in love until I was ten. She quietly slipped away on the day I took my eleven-plus.

She knew it was the end on that morning, wincing with pain as she attempted to lean forward to cup my smiling face between her hands, gently stroking me as if she was loathe ever to let go. Tears rolled unchecked down her beautiful face, her eyes as always exuding so much love for me, her mouth wreathed in a gentle smile. She bade me do well and make her proud of me. 'You are my life, my precious love, my very reason for living, my own very special chosen little girl. You must be a very brave one and never forget that Mummy will always be with you.'

I naturally thought she was referring to the impending exams.

In spite of all the upheavals, I went through in changes of addresses and thus having to change schools several times, I was a bright child and expected to pass the exams with ease. I kissed her goodbye, a smile, as always on my face, as I cheerfully left, little realising that it was for the last time and that a light was being extinguished in my life and it would never be quite the same again!

I rushed exuberantly out of school. I had found the exams easy and couldn't wait to report back to Mum…

A sombre Uncle Frank met me at the school gates with the news and took me to one or other of my aunts. I barely noticed which one. It didn't really sink in; Dad was there, his face ashen, eyes red-rimmed through crying.

'It's only the two of us now, we'll have to be strong for each other,' he whispered, hugging me tightly.

I knew, of course, that she had been very poorly but, with childish illogic, I had assumed that she would always be there for me with her sweet smile, her unstinting love in which she always enveloped me. I still expected to go home to find her, flop on the bed for a cuddle and tell her excitedly about my day.

The distinct 'coolness' in the air between Mum's grieving family and my father, was of course not at that time apparent to me. They were all there to give me the comfort and support that Louise would not have needed to ask of them.

Dad had been 'working away' at an American Air Force Base the other side of the country for quite a while before the bereavement occurred, travelling back for some weekends to see Louise and, of course, me (the burying-your-head-in-the-sand reaction, I guess). We hadn't seen a lot of him, so returning from hospital to the care of her family for the very last time, for those very precious remaining few weeks of her life the tender, loving care for Mum had come from her adoring family. I loved and cared for her too, to the best of my ability. She was forty-two, I was ten.

I didn't go to the funeral, perhaps they thought it inappropriate for a child and perhaps it was. Dad took me to see the flowers on the grave of which there were hundreds—seeming to me, a young child, to spread for miles.

Louise had been loved by so many people, family, friends, hospital staff, so these were their tributes to her: beautiful, bright colours, vibrant spring flowers, their wonderful scents pervading the air all around. I can smell them now, they were symbolic of everything she was, sweet and fresh and just simply divine, such a special person…I can see why God wanted her back early, enriching his life just as she had ours!

But standing there, next to my grieving father, the reality didn't really sink in. I was in truth far more concerned about the forthcoming wedding of my cousin Anne (eldest daughter of my holiday aunt & uncle) and my chance to be a bridesmaid for the first time; as a little girl of ten I guess this wasn't surprising.

Dad seemed to have returned permanently to our home and presumably to resume my care, and if I wondered why I wasn't as usual immersed in the midst of my aunts and uncles it didn't register in the confusion and sombre mood of everyone around me.

A very few days had elapsed after the burial when the first thunderbolt struck. Dad suggested over supper, that if I opted not to be a bridesmaid to my cousin, he would take me to Butlins!

Joy of joy, that wonderful mystic, exciting place that school friends talked about. I had always been so envious of them, so desperate to go, I had asked on many occasions, but with Louise so poorly, holidays were not an option for us as a family. I enjoyed day trips to the coast with Auntie Ciss and Nell, which were a lovely treat but coming a poor second! It never occurred to me to question why the choice, why the carrot was being dangled, but, nevertheless, the lure of the bridesmaid's dress and razzamatazz won. I had my moment of glory joining in the fun of a lovely family day.

Angered that he couldn't coerce me into changing my mind, Dad didn't join us for my cousin's wedding, and this was the last time for many years that I saw my loving relatives, other than for a fleeting hello in most unwelcoming circumstances. They, who had so willingly taken on the task of my well-being out of devotion to Louise, were no longer to feature in my life.

And we never did get to Butlins!

## —TWO—
## CHANGES

Life became different; Dad started work at the gas board as their safety officer and we led a bit of a hit-and-miss lifestyle.

He arrived home early evening from the office and I had to change role from child to housewife in my inimitable way, trying to take care of him.

I became rotund! We both had lunchtime meals out and so tea for me consisted of chocolate éclairs and other calorie-loaded delights that an over-sufficiency of money and a child's eye view of food entailed! My friends thought it wonderful, coming home with me to an empty house and eating the gourmet delights of the bakery and sweet shops! As long as I was happy, Dad seemed unaware of my dietary habits; he was immersed in his own world.

Visits to Louise's family didn't occur now. In the early days they regularly phoned; Dad was usually abrupt to them on the phone. Occasionally they came to the house but Dad was usually curt and unwelcoming and so they ceased coming. Instead visits to relatives, albeit fairly infrequently were now to his family.

They had always lurked dimly in the background but he had never had a close relationship with them; they hardly knew me and certainly held no delights for me either, rather the reverse. They were really virtual strangers to me and they came a very poor second to my beloved aunts and uncles on Louise's side, whom I was missing so very much.

Like Louise, Dad came from a big family, though not as large as Louise's. He was the youngest, the only boy, with a twin and four others sisters.

I had a nana that lived upstairs in the house of his twin sister and her family—a foreboding lady of indiscriminate age, but who seemed like Methuselah to me She washed her hair in Tide, a harsh soap powder, and her main preoccupation seemed to be wanting to pierce my ears with a needle, which she was always wielding with a glint in her eye. As she was nearly blind this thought terrified me and I cowered under the table the whole time we spent in the house, in sheer terror lest she carried out her threats. I wasn't a very brave soul! There were lots of cousins in the family and I am sure she had pierced all their ears for them, but she wasn't going near mine!

My granddad wasn't alive but I remember him as a kindly man who had once made me a doll's house, painstakingly carved out of wood. Dad's twin sister was a lovely lady too, almost on a par with my beloved other relatives on Louise's side. I had stayed with her very occasionally (they had one boy around my age and we enjoyed a good camaraderie, both of us only children—

we shared vivid imaginations and invented some wonderful games together). Her husband fell very far short of these criteria though; he used to follow me upstairs and try and corner me on the landing on my way to the toilet to practise the art of French kissing. Naïve as I was, and only a very young child, I knew this was wrong and managed to stay out of his way, exercising twenty-four-hour bladder control. Surprisingly, I never told anyone of this (probably because I didn't have anyone to tell) and I kept the secret for years until an adult. It would have broken my aunt's heart.

Fortunately, our paths crossed very rarely, but even as an adult when we met up he could never look me in the eye, and I couldn't bear to look at him either; he must have wondered if I was ever going to drop him in it. He still made me feel sick in the pit of my stomach.

In those days we would have labelled him a dirty old man but in this day and age, when we are so much more enlightened about these things, a more sinister name I guess. I hope he didn't try the same thing with other cousins in the family. I often wondered, for he saw them a great deal more often than he saw me.

There were other aunts and uncles on Dad's side, but we had never seemed to mix with them, on reflection probably because of my total involvement with Mum's side of the family. In contrast to the welcoming love they had cocooned me in, Dad's family seemed not to consider me a part of the family; they didn't do the same things for me as my other cousins, maybe because I was adopted. I never really knew or, to be honest, cared. After Louise's death they still remained distant figures in my life.

My two most vivid memories of them included one of Auntie Gladys, who had a B & B in Southend. I think we visited her twice. I was mesmerised by the fact that she washed her smalls in the washing-up water in the sink; to this day I'm still not sure whether it was before or after she did the washing-up for her boarders!! I have a more than sneaking suspicion it was the former! She was a very heavy smoker and used to stand by the stove, cigarette in her mouth, leaning over the bacon and eggs sizzling in the frying pan, with the ash getting longer and longer, poised to drop off straight into the eggs. I used to hold my breath in morbid fascination, willing it to fall in, but somehow she always seemed to avoid the catastrophe…or perhaps she didn't! She was a typical seaside landlady, of the sort you see as the butt of comediennes' jokes. I could just see her, hands on hips, scarf around her head giving out the house rules… . It would have taken a brave soul to cross swords with her.

The second memory was of Auntie Rene, although not so much her, as what she did for a living. Together with spouse, they had an undertakers shop in Kensington. They lived in a flat above the workshop or whatever you call the place where they have people lying in coffins awaiting burial (I don't think they had Chapels of Rest in undertakers' premises then as we do now). Unfortunately the only toilet was downstairs on the ground floor, passing the room which housed the bodies and the coffins; wild horses wouldn't have dragged me down there. I had a very fertile imagination, not helped by my dad telling me tales that the place was haunted! I declined to drink anything, was convinced I saw things move and heard eerie noises, sat terrified, cross-legged under the table, praying it would soon be time to go home and when we eventually did, I was so relieved that we had to stop somewhere for me to go behind the bushes, for a wee, much to the amusement of my father.

I think we visited once but nothing could persuade me to make a repeat visit.

Life for me wasn't unhappy though, lonely possibly. As with many only children I had the most vivid imagination and when I wasn't eating, I immersed myself in books and writing stories. Dad was an articulate, cultured man, a lover of books, an author and he loved to paint. Although adopted, strangely I seemed to have inherited these talents from him. His other great love was fishing and we regularly did really 'exciting' things like going to fishing matches or re-stocking lakes, and so on. Unfortunately I was never dextrous, nor had any coordination, so most of these excursions ended with my falling down murky river banks, mud-splattered and with sodden clothes, my rotund backside protruding from the waters… . Dad resignedly had to abandon what he was doing to take me home! Which I was always pleased about, but after a while he got wise to this and took spare sets of clothes with him. All good, girlie-type fun!!

Dad treated me like a companion rather than a child and I suppose it would be true to say I developed an old head on young shoulders.

My most cherished possession in the entire world was a little dog called Waggy. A matter of days after Louise died, we had spotted him wandering around, tail between his legs, dejected. Mooching around the gardens of the houses where we lived, obviously a stray or someone's unwanted pet, I had implored Dad to 'take him in'.

We followed all of the correct procedures of course: notifying the police, the local dogs' home; and I waited, almost holding my breath, for someone to claim him, praying desperately they wouldn't.

My prayers were answered and he became mine, someone upon whom I could lavish my love, share my days with, a real ragamuffin, and a bundle of fun bringing me untold joy. Maybe, if you believe in destiny, it was Louise watching over me, seeing the hurt I was going through, who gave him a gentle nudge in the direction of our garden. She would have known what a special place he would have in my heart.

A real ragamuffin, full of fun and mischief, I absolutely adored him and where I went Waggy went too. I had to be prised apart from him even to go to school.

## —THREE—
## WARNING BELLS

The first nail in my coffin, so to speak, was when Dad informed me that I was to meet a friend of his…a lady whom he had met whilst working in Lancashire at the airforce base. He wanted me to stay with her and her mother for a week to, in his words 'get acquainted with one another'. Her name, he said, was Alice. He didn't volunteer any more information and I didn't think to ask.

I was excited; the prospect of an adventure, a holiday with nice kindly people had great appeal and my imagination was already ahead of me. It was in fact only a matter of months since Mum had died and on the surface things were 'normal' at home, Dad and I being in a routine of sorts. As eccentric as it might have seemed by other people's standards, it would be nice to see some new faces and I missed my family very much…

Dad took me to this delightful little cottage in Newton Le Willows, a picturesque little village in Lancashire where Alice, together with her mother lived and I was dropped off with the promise of being collected the following week. I was very upset as Waggy had to be left at home because they didn't like dogs apparently, which was beyond my childlike comprehension. I had argued the point with Dad; how could anyone not like a bundle of mischief? He didn't have fleas, didn't wee in the house but Dad was not budging an inch, it was, he said, 'a time for us all to get to know each other' and Waggy wasn't part of the equation.

If there was a great bond between Dad and these people it certainly wasn't apparent to me as an eleven-year-old child for he didn't waste any time in getting away, giving me a brief hug as he departed in what appeared to be unseemly haste, given that I had never met these people before.

Alice was a tall slim lady, who, although she was much younger, had hair seeming to me to be already going white like my nana's. I didn't give her a lot of thought really; I suppose she was ordinary, not beautiful as my beloved mum had been. I did notice though that, when she smiled, which seemed to be infrequently (although as her mother seemed always to be shouting at her perhaps she didn't have that much to smile about!) it didn't light up her face with warmth. It didn't make her eyes and her wrinkles twinkle and her chin wobble—that's what I had been used to with my family of aunts and uncles. It amounted to an empty gesture, never moving beyond her mouth.

Her mother didn't seem to smile at all…after the first couple of minutes of meeting her I had christened her the

'Wicked Witch'. I'd never really met anyone quite like her before—with her steely grey eyes and grim expression, I was surreptitiously looking around for her broomstick and her cat. She would have made my ear-piercing nana look like the Christmas tree fairy!

They lived in a picture-postcard setting, next to a water tower, the railway line running beneath only yards away. My fertile imagination had already run riot into a fantasy world reminiscent of the *Railway Children* and I was itching to get out and about and play.

In spite of my involvement with make-believe, it quickly became apparent even to me that this wasn't a 'normal' happy household, as I, a child, knew it. Alice, whom I now know to have been about thirty-three, was completely dominated by her mother who seemed to make her life a living misery. She (Alice) was a lady of very nervous disposition. (I learnt later that she had had several breakdowns, no doubt brought about by the attitude of her mother towards her.) Row after row erupted in the house, with Alice threatening to throw herself off the nearby viaduct. I didn't understand the reasons for the rows; Alice's mother, always abusive, always instigated them. Of course, to me this made no sense whatsoever and as it was completely new territory I was utterly bewildered.

I'd had no experience of this sort of environment where words were never spoken gently but only harshly and with malice of thought. And tears were more predominant than any other emotion; it was all totally alien to me.

The week passed, yet I had no opportunity to get to know anyone; I was fed and attended to, mostly by the Wicked Witch, Alice's mother as I had christened her, but never talked to and laughed with and I was certainly tolerated rather than welcomed. I spent all my days from first thing in the morning until dusk, playing outside by the side of the railway embankment, making pretend signs, waving to passengers on the trains, writing stories. There were many occasions when I was really homesick because of all the rows and wished I was on one of those trains myself going home, but, with the resilience of a child, I awaited Dad's arrival to convey me back to my beloved Waggy.

When he arrived, it was the first time in the entire week that peace had prevailed in the house; there was no bickering and everyone seemed on their best behaviour. With everyone present, Dad informed me that I was to have a new mother, that Alice and her mother (the Wicked Witch in my thoughts—only he referred to her much more politely!) would be coming to make their home with us and we would all be one big happy family…

I was pretty surprised, I'd not had an inkling, and Alice hadn't spent any time getting to know me, as one would perhaps have expected with a prospective new stepdaughter. She seemed relieved that I had been out of the way most of the time.

This was six months after the death of Louise, and, notwithstanding that enormity, the dramas of the past week evaporated into a child's innocent excitement at a wedding…and yes, a mum too! Living with a man as preoccupied as Dad, in spite of his good intentions, for a young lady entering her teenage years with no feminine influences around, wasn't that easy. I harboured absolutely no misgivings, only genuine excitement, thrilled at the thought of a new mum to share my life with and I rushed over to give her a hug which, if it was not reciprocated, I didn't notice, being on cloud nine myself.

I had adored Louise, but because of her illness we had not for almost all of the years I could remember, been able to do mum-and-daughter type things together as my friends at school did. I don't think we ever went out shopping or on an outing. It hadn't worried me a jot then; she was my world in whatever form it took, but now the prospect of being able to do these things, having a mum to share secrets with, like my friends did, having someone to talk to and help me through the girlie things that I felt I couldn't talk to Dad about seemed wonderful. (For example, I had carried the secret of the onset of my period around with me for several months, stuffing wads of toilet roll in my knickers, convinced that I had some dreadful disease. It was just wonderful when some slightly more worldly school chum had explained it to me.)

Frankly, I was naïve: I missed the warmth of my aunts' care and attention lavished on me in the past, and the hope that I could rekindle this affection with someone else was something to really look forward to. I was a child with so much love to give. A real Friday's Child!

A wedding meant 'another' bridesmaid's dress! Unbridled joy! Alice and the Wicked Witch accompanied by Dad's eldest and wealthiest sister, dour Auntie Wyn, who had dairy businesses in Chiswick (with hindsight one assumed she was contributing to the cost), did the rounds of bridal shops for the works… . It seemed it was going to be a 'proper' wedding with all the trimmings and no expense spared.

My Auntie Wyn did not like children in any shape or form so this was not a fun outing; children were to be seen and not heard, I didn't know her and she clearly had no wish to get better acquainted with me! With my customary vivid imagination, I had already cast her as a likely wife of the Child Catcher in *Chitty Chitty Bang Bang*. Looking covertly at her from under my eyelashes, my overactive imagination was already in gear thinking of what gory end could befall her! But nothing could spoil this day.

As my round little body was pushed and pummelled into ill-fitting flock nylon bridesmaids' dresses (all those cakes and sweets, remember) and various headdresses of forget-me-knots, roses and others were plonked askew on top of my rotund little face (my waist was bigger than my bosoms so the dresses I tried on were all much too big for me overall in order to fit my waistline!), I really looked like 'Orphan Annie' in her big sister's clothes, but I was in ecstasy. Throughout the exercise, my aunt tutted and frowned and told me to keep still and be quiet…and only the vision of 'her' tied up in the great big net with the children swarming all over her kept me going! My feet were crammed into dainty ballerina-like shoes and I really thought I'd died and gone to heaven! Alice herself had said very little, trying on dress after dress and eventually one was chosen, for her and for me. Auntie Wyn led the way and she complied. There was no banter between us, no camaraderie on what should have been a lovely day for us all.

The ugly duckling image notwithstanding, I was content. We were treated to lunch by my aunt who insisted that I sat next to her—'to keep an eye on you'. And she told me, 'Don't speak with your mouth full, sit up, don't slouch, take your elbow off the table'—this was followed by her knocking it with long Cruella-like fingers. 'Children should be seen and not heard, speak up, don't mumble, chew your food...' I really couldn't win so I retreated into my own fantasy world and prayed that a caterpillar would crawl up out of her dinner into the fur stole that remained draped around her shoulder, or, better still, into her mouth. Very posh, my Auntie Wyn! She even gave the very smart black-dressed, frilly-pinnied waitress five whole shillings. That would have kept Waggy in dog food for weeks.

Meal ended, and laden with our packages, we made our weary way home with my insisting on carrying all of my new possessions myself. I had to be dissuaded from trying on and wearing the bridesmaid's shoes on the underground; the crowded tube my catwalk! I was so excited and thrilled.

Preparations over all too quickly, the wedding took place... . I think it was in Lancashire, but if the truth were known, I cannot remember a single thing about it. I don't think any family or people known to me came. Unfortunately my mind has blanked this period of my life out as the onset of my darkest days. Perhaps a psychologist would be able to illustrate why...I never saw one. My only recall was that they had a couple of days' honeymoon in Southport, but who cared for me I have no recall; it certainly wasn't the Wicked Witch.

# —FOUR—
# BEGINNINGS

Following the wedding and brief honeymoon, Alice *and* the WW moved lock, stock and barrel into the house that Dad and I had shared with Louise in South Ealing. The WW was something I hadn't bargained for. I had been told, but hadn't taken on board that she was a part of the deal and I had naively imagined that life would be with Dad, Alice and myself, as a happy little trio, living happily ever after.

I still knew nothing about Alice: we had no conversations as such, let alone a rapport, her time seemed to be solely directed in pacifying the demands of her mother.

I had fantasised that that was why she was marrying Dad: to escape, and that once this was fulfilled she would become warm and loving to me. Some hope! That was all I wanted really, what I suppose all little girls want, a mum to love me.

They moved into our home; it was exciting, ferrying all of the boxes in and I chattered non-stop, so looking forward to the reinstatement of the warm happy atmosphere there had always been there whilst Mum and her family were about. The house was exactly as when Mum was there, her knick-knacks remained in situ (well, those which my Dad's sisters hadn't fought over and removed after her death in an undignified rugby scrum, together with her clothes and jewellery). There was no attempt by Dad to clear the decks, so to speak, to enable Alice to make her mark; and the family photographs and mementoes still adorned the mantelpiece, even the bedding was the same. I don't think Dad intended this as a slight to Alice; he just didn't think!

The removal men finished at last, on that very first evening. It was the start of our new life together as a family, belongings sorted as much as they could be: much of WW's furniture and belongings had moved with them into an already full house; so the whole place resembled a giant second-hand furniture store with things jammed in everywhere in higgledy-piggledy chaos. Dad suggested that he and Alice might go out for a while, a reasonable request I guess as I suppose technically they were on honeymoon still.

However, the Wicked Witch was having none of it... . Accusations that they had uprooted her to be a glorified babysitter abounded and a tirade of abuse followed. Dad was completely aghast; he had never witnessed any such scenes before (yet I knew them to be commonplace). He tried to remonstrate with her but it fell on deaf ears.

Two hours later, with everyone in the house reduced to a gibbering wreck except WW, she suggested that we all might like to kneel by the fireguard and repent our sins!!

Alice meekly complied; I knew this to be commonplace too. Dad and I gave each other shell-shocked glances (I had been bawling for most of this time in sheer confusion) and he left the house. I disappeared up to my room.

That little room, and the subsequent one when we moved house a few months later to Hounslow, became my sanctuary, not free from intrusion but at least somewhere that I could, albeit temporarily, escape the reality and dream instead.

Life was a nightmare for all: Alice must have conceived almost immediately and she lurched through the early months of pregnancy poorly and most definitely clinically depressed. She was very far removed from the normal concept of a new bride and a soon-to-be mum.

Just as when she lived at home, the rows were a daily occurrence but the pattern changed. Obviously from the moment Dad and I left the house in the mornings for workplace and school respectively, the WW held court—with her verbal abuse directed at Alice.

It never stopped and she treated her like her personal slave.

Totally bombastic, dominating the household, there were no choices for Alice or recognition that this was her home. Housework was regimental: Monday was washing day, Tuesday was Ironing, Wednesday Bedrooms, Thursday Sitting Room, and so on, never deviated from. The same applied to meals: Monday lunchtime was tripe cooked in milk (so I never ate on Mondays if I happened to be in the house!), Tuesday Shepherd's Pie. I can't remember the others but they never varied on their set day. Sundays were always roast lamb, cabbage and rice pudding.

Tea was regimented too; no variation whatsoever—always cooked meat i.e. one slice of ham or tongue, a tomato, bread and butter and a cake, this last being whatever was on offer at the local shop as baking didn't feature in the household routine. There was never enough to eat. The WW controlled everything with Alice meekly complying; it was as if they were in a time warp.

Lurching through pregnancy, there was no scope for choices for her; nothing had changed for Alice in her move except that she now had a husband and child to contend with. It was all too much for her. She couldn't pretend Dad wasn't around but she certainly could with me in those early days. Dad spent much of his time out of the house anyway; he had reverted to eating a main meal at work at lunchtimes but his calorie intake was so drastically reduced that he became much leaner and was forever hungry, foraging for non-existent biscuits and filler-uppers in the empty cupboards.

Like Dad, I suddenly began to really 'enjoy' school dinners. A picky eater before, I now devoured everything in sight. Instead of the rotund little pudding I had been before, I now became a literal beanpole earning the dubious title of Olive Oil from my peers at school.

Alice was a compliant slave to WW as she had obviously always been; any hopes of breaking away and independence (if indeed she had ever harboured that ambition) through marriage definitely not occurring. Dad spent less and less time at home, working longer hours, involved with fishing clubs, any excuse he could muster. He was completely out of his depth with the aggression in the house.

In my case, however, I had to return from school into

the 'Lion's Den'. Things subtly, or maybe not so subtly changed; whatever nightmares had taken place in the daytime between the two of them transposed themselves to me when I walked in that door. I became the focus of Alice's attentions, not in the nice way I had so longed for but in the way that was to mark the beginning of the end for me—the ruination of my life. Now Alice no longer was the victim but the perpetrator, not the bullied but the bully.

Over a short period of time, I no longer represented to her someone who came as part of the baggage surrounding Dad (as I felt she had considered me), but the object of all her frustrations and anger and probably, with hindsight, disillusionment. Where she was subservient to her mother she now used me as a vessel to discharge all of the emotions she felt...

It started with verbal abuse: a tirade of meaningless aggression used to hit me as I entered the door, what I had, what I hadn't done, what a useless specimen I was, how I was the reason for all of the unhappiness in the house, how much 'they' (never enlarged upon as to who) hated me and how I was spoiling their lives.

I was twelve years old, a sunny uncomplicated child, bright, outgoing, desperate to be loved I guess. Throughout my life people had warmed to me with my endearing qualities, extrovert nature and affectionate manner. Now suddenly, and quite inexplicably to me, this had all changed. I was so confused. I reasoned that I had to be doing something very bad to make her so angry with me all of the time. I didn't understand what, but I tried so very hard to please Alice, to buy affection through deeds, that even a little warmth or affection, a smile, a gentle word would have done.

There was a jumble sale being held in our local hall. As the doors were opened and people surged in, making a beeline for the mountains of clothes and cake stalls, toys and books, all piled up higgledy-piggledy in exciting chaos, something guided me away from my usual assault on the piles of books, usually my only motive for attending, my escape into the magical world of words and fantasy. My few pennies of saved-up pocket money seemed to go a long way towards keeping me in books, at least until the next event. Instead, I headed towards the biggest stall of all—piled table to ceiling with an array of colourful clothing, catering for every size and taste. From this cornucopia of garments, I spotted the most wonderful fox stole; a cry of ecstasy rang from my mouth as its glassy eyes said, 'Buy me for Alice, she'll be so pleased to be as posh as Auntie Wyn and she'll be bound to be happy with you.' And minutes later, having proffered my two shillings to the round, wobbly lady behind the table, and pleaded with her, as she asked for much more money, that I just knew I had to have it for my mum, my joy knew no bounds. I rushed out into the wintry sunlight, with foxy clutched under my arm. I was unable to contain myself from running as fast as my legs would carry me to deliver my gift, quivering with excitement:

"Mum."

"Don't call me that, I'm not your mother," came from Alice.

Even that though was not enough to deter me. "Look what I've brought you, just like Auntie Wyn, so that you can wear it with a posh frock when you go out," and proffering the stole, "Isn't it lovely?"

"You disgusting, disgusting creature. Bringing that flea-ridden thing in here. It's about as bad as that smelly dog of yours. You did it on purpose to bring fleas into the house! You are a wicked evil child."

With that, it was wrenched out of my arms with such force that it sent me reeling backwards, and the stole was hurled by the tip of its tail into the Rayburn Stove, the flames engulfing it in seconds, and with it a part of my heart.

I huddled upstairs in the sanctuary of my room, weeping copiously, wondering what I had done wrong, for I surely didn't know and I had only wanted so badly to please…

It was one of many rebuffs which I took on board in those first few months. This onslaught, and the many others that were forthcoming with ever increasing regularity, I bore with the resilience of a child, making sure I did everything that was asked of me as quietly and as quickly as possible so as not to invoke a reaction. I tackled escalating lists of chores, trying so hard to please, to be helpful: in short, anything to keep the peace.

The peace was never kept however… . Whatever had taken place in the house between Alice and the WW, during Dad's and my absence, the subsequent onslaught of verbal abuse that I faced daily upon my return from school, my stomach churning in apprehension as I opened the door, all this faded into insignificance with the row that was guaranteed to erupt when Dad walked through that door in the evenings.

It became like a deadly game of charades. For the

purpose of the plot Alice and the WW who had been at each other's throats all day, joined forces to become conspirators in holding court.

As my father's key turned in the lock, I was frog-marched from wherever or whatever I was doing and made to stand in front of my father where he was acquainted with my seemingly endless list of misdemeanours, rudeness, lack of co-operation. I was belittled, a tissue of lies erupting from them both. In those early days I was completely bewildered by all this fantasy. But I quickly realised it was pointless to try and defend myself as it would have been impossible to get a word in edgeways anyway even if I had wanted to and, more to the point, I felt sure that my father was astute enough to realise the absurdity of it all.

Astute he may have been, but completely out of his depth he most certainly was. In those early days he defended me rigorously, chiding gently that he felt sure things weren't as bad as they were portrayed... . Talk about a red rag to a bull! I am sure the screams and shouts could have been heard on the other side of Hounslow; on several occasions we had visits from the police after neighbours had complained about the noise.

The outcome was always the same, when the onslaught had 'blown' itself out and Dad had declined to join the prayer forgiveness session by the fireguard, he and I would spend the rest of the evening in stony silence in one room whilst Alice and the WW ensconced themselves in the other. Most of the time now we didn't eat in the evenings because the rows erupted as he walked in the door.

At this time the thing that meant the most to me in the whole wide world, Waggy, disappeared.

I was curtly told that it was 'God's punishment' to me for being so wicked; he had been unwell and had had to be put to sleep. He had been fine when I left for school in the morning… . I was utterly distraught, crying myself to sleep for days; he had been my one friend in this house of horror.

༄

Into this uneasy household, my sister was born. I was so thrilled; like so many only children I had longed for siblings and the arrival of this little baby was a joy to my heart, even eclipsing the unhappiness that I was going through. The love and warmth I experienced towards my sister has continued throughout my life but in those early days after her birth when Alice returned to the house and I was desperate to get to know her, to hold and cherish her, I was quickly and curtly told not to get any ideas; that 'she' was no relation to me and I was not going to corrupt her with my evil ways. I was only adopted, not a part of their family, and my father only continued to look after me out of the goodness of his heart, not wanting me as he had his own little girl now.

Alice, clinically depressed throughout the pregnancy, was even more so now in the aftermath of birth and the need to care for a baby. Dad, following his induction into the inexplicable way of life of his new marriage, withdrew even more into a distant figure, seldom around.

In his mid-forties, with a shrew for a wife and a mother-in-law from hell, a young baby and, last but not least, an adoptive daughter he could see deteriorating before his eyes, he couldn't handle any of it so he just closed his eyes to them, burying his head in the sand and hoping they would all go away. Any excuse he could find to get himself out of the house became something of paramount importance not to be missed.

Nothing got better. Astonishingly Alice was pregnant again…a month after the birth of Elizabeth. WW wasted no time in belittling the foolhardiness of this (personally, in later life I have come to the conclusion it must have been an immaculate conception, for Dad and Alice barely spoke to each other with civility, never mind going through the motions of conceiving a child, but there you go). She was receiving treatment for depression but it seemed to be making no inroads. Fate had dealt a cruel blow in this latest pregnancy. It was to prove to be a turning point in the pattern of what had become my unhappy life.

# ―FIVE―
# Disillusionment

In a very short space of time, the verbal bullying that went on around the clock towards me took on other more sinister meaning. Slowly but surely Alice contrived to undermine everything I did. I was no longer allowed to go out after school with friends or even to ask a friend around. The explanation I was given was that I had too many jobs to do and never did them properly. I ceased to have any leisure time when I could give free rein to my imagination and immerse myself in my books or even to do my homework from school.

My modest pocket money that Dad gave me on a weekly basis was, as soon as he had moved out of earshot, confiscated so that I never had any money for anything. Excuses for this behaviour were cunningly contrived to put me in the wrong, i.e. that I was taking money from Alice's purse, keeping change from shopping, etc.— completely false accusations, for such actions wouldn't have even occurred to me.

Other limitations were also placed on me; I was no longer allowed to go to St John's Ambulance and the Girls Life Brigade as I had for several years, and had really loved. I was always told it was because I was slovenly and never did the jobs properly and needed to do them again and again. I hadn't the money for the weekly subscriptions anyway. At school too, anything I needed money for or wanted to do caused a major furore, and I knew better than to ask for money to go on school trips, let alone school holidays that my friends went on, which were always denied me.

The reasons for this were always so plausibly given by Alice and WW in those early days before I was too weary even to argue and used to go to my father, that I almost began to question my sanity. Was I really doing all those awful things, was I the terrible child that they were so quick to accuse me of being?

Apart from school, the only time I actually left the house was to take my sister up and down the road in her pram, always being admonished not to dare come back if anything happened to her! Usually going only as far as the local shop, it got so that I was terrified of even this seemingly innocent chore.

I was cowed, completely introverted, frightened even to speak for fear of the onslaught, often physically sick now on my way home from school in sheer apprehension of what I would face. I had convinced myself that I was 'The Child of the Devil' so evil did I believe myself to be…

I suppose it was only a question of time before the round-the-clock verbal abuse became physical.

Ours was a very volatile, violent household now. We no longer sat together in different rooms, my father was deflated, he nearly always went out or upstairs, if he bothered to come home at all until late in the evening. I looked for whatever sanctuary I could, and usually in vain.

I recall that after one of the usual evening outbursts, I was upstairs in my room when I heard a terrible hubbub followed by screams emanating from my father and Alice's room. I entered, only to find my passive-natured father sitting astride a heavily pregnant Alice, hitting out with brutal intensity to her very obvious terror. I sprang (totally illogically it would seem, looking back) to her defence, trying to pull my father off.

In all my life, I had never known my father—a scholarly man who would always use words in preference to anything else—display an iota of aggression. Something within him had obviously just snapped and he had been pushed beyond his limits of endurance.

Verbal aggression had, as awful as it sounds to admit it, become a way of life for me now and I guess it had always been only a question of time before this was taken a step further.

It started with pushing me out of the way, from rooms, through doorways, and so on, the odd slap across the face, hands jammed in drawers, that kind of thing.

At first, these episodes met with very temporary contrition, caused, I think by a fear that I would tell my father. I did…but things had grown increasingly difficult in that quarter.

The birth of his son had called for a temporary euphoria in the house…the keeping of the family name and all that (he was the only boy with five sisters, remember, so his birth had been heralded with rejoicing, he was keeping up with the tradition). Dad was over the moon, and for a short while surpassed himself in being a doting husband and father, to the babies anyway...

The days of being a doting father to me had long since passed, I'm afraid, he wanted an easy life and so if that involved being seen to endorse that I was the 'black sheep of the family', then so be it. Whilst not abusive to me himself, it was as if I was invisible, didn't exist and he turned his back on the anguish I was going through.

My punishment for being there in their space was to overlap into other areas.

I no longer had new clothes, my school uniform was now looking very scruffy. I walked to school a distance of several miles, my school friends cycled. I grovelled, pleaded to Dad for a bike (I never had the courage to ask Alice for anything) for many years to no avail. Everything I needed for school, even simple things like domestic science ingredients caused a major row, and most of the time I just pretended I had forgotten them. The row I got into at school was nothing compared to the problems of asking for things at home. We were comfortable; my father earned a good salary so finances were not a problem—it was just me they were unprepared to spend anything on. Items for needlework, and so on were like asking for the sun, moon and stars. During the whole time I was at a senior school, I made the same pair of pyjamas with the most awful winceyette, tiny polka dot material that Alice had purchased for me just after their marriage. The fabric used to give me double vision and how I loathed it! The pins rusted into the material. I couldn't bring myself to do anything with it, but in spite of the teacher's numerous requests, I was never allowed to move on to something more appropriate.

On the home front, we never went anywhere either. Alice had an intense dislike of travel and indeed pretty much of leaving the house, bordering on a phobia, so we never had family excursions. I doubt I would have been included even if they had. She loathed me so much that she really didn't want to breathe the same air as me and I spent much of the time holding my breath in her presence in case she noticed me and I had to face the repercussions...

The gilt had gone off the gingerbread again in the parenting role as far as Dad was concerned. My brother, unlike my sister was a difficult child, always crying, never sleeping. He obviously picked up the vibes of this house of trauma.

Alice never recovered from her depression and must have had (with hindsight) a most difficult life with WW dominating her. I was the scapegoat upon whom she vented her frustrations.

The odd slaps became heavier; they were accompanied by hair-pulling, crescendos of hysteria when I would be dragged from room to room, my head repeatedly banged on walls, pushed under water in the bathroom, crashed against the taps, kicked. There was no contrition any more, just inane jealousy and hate. It seemed that it was unacceptable to her that I should be a part of my father's life. Now not only was I always being verbally harassed, but my body became a fusion of cuts and bruises, aches and discomfort. I was almost at the point of no return. I tried to talk to my father but he just said I was exaggerating, and didn't want to know.

The doctor diagnosed alopaecia when I was taken to him because my hair was falling out. I wanted to scream at him, 'Spend half an hour a day being dragged around by your hair and see what happens to yours…!' But I said nothing, I was afraid to.

My life was a misery. I was no longer the happy extrovert child. It was not going unnoticed. My only salvation was school where I could lose myself in my thirst for knowledge, in books that I devoured as if they were going out of print. The danger signals were there but nobody read them, my silent pleas for help. They were silent. Somehow I felt that this must be all down to me. My lot. Something I had done in my life but I didn't know what.

I desperately wanted the love of my aunts and uncles; I thought that they would help me but my self-esteem was so low that I convinced myself they probably wouldn't want to know either. Besides this, we had moved and I had no way of reaching them and no money. I never went out, although by now I had resorted to doing the very thing that I had been unjustly accused of, stealing money from Alice's purse, but only in sufficient quantities to buy myself toiletries and sanitary towels, and so on. I wrote to Mum's sisters craving affection but did not tell them of my plight. I prayed they would read between the lines, be telepathic enough to see what I wasn't brave enough to write.

A couple of days before Christmas they, Auntie Ciss and Auntie Nell, came to the house. I think, although they didn't say, it was in response to my letter. They had brought me Christmas presents, and my Auntie Gwen had knitted me a jumper. They were treated courteously but very coolly. This was the first time they had met Alice. They said they had written and sent me gifts through the post. I hadn't received them. They weren't asked in, they were made to feel very unwelcome and sadly they never returned. Dad wasn't there. They later told me how very shocked they were at my appearance compared to the plump jolly little girl they had known and loved.

The door closed behind them with a decisive click. I was filled with a sense of foreboding. I knew it so well—the strange, sweet yet salty taste of fear welling up in my nostrils and mouth; my heart seeming to beat so fast it would burst...

Alice turned from the doorway, I made a last-ditch attempt to duck past her in the hallway to get up the stairs but I knew it was pointless.

She pulls me into the front room, catching my ankle as she slams the door behind us with such ferocity. Involuntarily, I start to wet myself. She is standing in front of the door. There is no escape. My desperate eyes dart around to look for somewhere to gain some scant protection.

Too late, she grabs my hair: 'You asked them to come and spy on us.'

'I didn't I didn't... please don't...'

'Don't what, you piece of garbage?' she screamed, dragging me towards the sideboard, smashing my head against the wall. 'They don't know what an evil bitch you are, incarnate of the devil.'

Hitting me, kicking me, digging her nails into my shoulder, I can taste blood, I can smell it, my head is swimming, round and round, my knees are giving way. No, no, please god; I fight to stay conscious.

Blood is running down my face: 'I'm sorry, please, please don't… it's all my fault. I did it, I'm bad, I'm wicked, and I told them to come, only please, please don't…'

Her hand is tightening around my throat, she is still kicking, and her anger knows no bounds. I am able to stand no longer, I have no fight left in me to try and survive. My body sinks into the merciful release of unconsciousness

When I come round, maybe seconds, maybe minutes or hours later—who knows—I am lying in my own urine, my battered body, bruised, bleeding and aching. I haven't the coordination of my limbs to move. Mercifully, I am alone.

'Mum, why have you forsaken me?'

# −Six−
# Devious Strategies

*T*here were a few highs as well as the multitude of lows. My very best friend in the world was a girl called Susie. She was plump, or curvaceous was probably the right word. She had the bust that we all coveted…even wearing a brassiere and she was very worldly. Her home life was very informal, bordering on unorthodox and I lived my life through her.

She was everything I had been—outgoing, gregarious, sunny, always looking for mischief. What she saw in me, a cowed, naïve, beanpole of gawky teenage years I'll never know, but she was my champion and, I have to say, my salvation.

It frustrated Susie that I wasn't allowed out except to take the children for a walk and she was always hatching plots to facilitate my escape for a few hours. I had mentioned the WW and Alice's obsession with religion and so she formulated a plan. Implementing this, it came about that I asked to be confirmed (with Susie). This was agreed and duly went ahead which meant I got out to attend communion classes on a weekly basis, always dawdling back, but the best was yet to come.

There are certain days in the year I believe when, taken to the letter, those newly confirmed should take communion. Susie researched this and so impressed the teachers with her knowledge and request for absenteeism to attend communion that they agreed and this was our excuse for some deliriously 'free' days. On these short occasions we did everything teenage girls of that era did…namely window-shopping and making a nuisance of themselves and, delight of all delights, cycling. I hadn't got a bike; Susie had a new and an old one, the latter which to my delirious joy she lent me. We hatched our plot of going off for a ride—simple enough, one would have assumed but: a) I was not a proficient cyclist by any stretch of the imagination, never having ridden a bike! And b) Susie's choice of venue for this ride in her usual inimitable style was the Great West Road. Admittedly it had a cycle track but the road was the nearest thing in the late fifties and early sixties to the M25!

We cycled, or, rather, I wobbled along with a complete lack of dexterity, my ecstasy knowing no bounds. I had not a care in the world until we unfortunately hit a kerb… a deep kerb. Susie dismounted, as any normal person would do…I jammed the brakes on! The bike went up in the air somehow, the saddle between my legs and I fell badly, pouring blood. Susie flagged down a passing motorist who called an ambulance…

The depth of my injuries was unknown but the sheer terror of being found out, exposed to Alice for being out enjoying myself on a cycle ride, eclipsed everything else and I wished I was dead! I was taken to a local cottage hospital, my injuries were superficial—bruises everywhere and lacerations to my vagina, I believe.

Susie had to call my father to get me... . To this day I don't know what she said...a grim-faced Dad collected me but God must have been on my side because the incident, after he brought me home, was not brought up and I was tucked up in bed by him with something approaching the old warmth and concern. I was in seventh heaven; it was almost worth the trauma and the pain to be treated in a kindly manner.

༄

Excursions were banned other than when I took the babies out. Lizzie would sit on a seat on the top of the awkward big coach pram and there was always a screaming baby inside for he just never stopped... . I was sent out with them just to give everyone a bit of peace from the incessant racket but it was a regular routine.

I was always escorted through the front door with the curt message, 'Don't bother coming back if anything happens to them—your life won't be worth living!' Susie usually met up with me in the recreation ground half a mile down the road. Here we would put the babies on the baby swings and I would sit next to Susie, listening to the stories of her various conquests while drooling at the mouth...lost in my own little world of make-believe. Gently rocking backwards and forwards on the swing was the only time my brother was ever quiet; he loved the swing.

On one of these occasions though, my brother fell out of the swing onto the concrete beneath, screaming even more ferociously that usual. In sheer terror and panic, with the dire warnings ringing in my ears of what would happen to me if anything happened to them, I carried him in my arms (Susie pushing the pram), trying to stop the crescendo. There was no visible sign of injury but I couldn't shut him up, try desperately as I might. I stood by the local shop, closer to home than was safe for comfort and certainly far too close for Susie to be seen with me, rocking him and trying to soothe him.

Crash, his head hit the plate-glass window of the shop with a resounding wallop. He stopped crying, obviously unconscious, but I didn't think of that. I bundled him into the pram, thanking God for my reprieve and trundled him home.

I placed the pram carefully in the front room where it was quiet, checking that he was asleep, which was usually the reason for my taking him out because, in addition to incessant crying, he never slept either.

One hour passed into two, two into three, Alice was amazed he was sleeping so long; I didn't have the courage to tell her what had occurred. When she wasn't around or in earshot, I rushed to the pram, lifting him out and shaking him like a rag doll but still he didn't waken!

For once in my life I didn't have to be told to pray. I was terrified. I didn't know what I feared the most—the prospect of there being anything wrong with David or the repercussions on me. Alice and the WW were suspicious! Thank God, after about four hours he awoke still crying. The poor little fellow must have had the most almighty headache but I didn't dare confess and to this day he still doesn't know. Sorry, David, although I did reveal all to my sister a couple of years ago. I never took him out of the pram again, and swings were definitely out!

Susie was my benefactor, we knew better than to attempt any such misdemeanours again but she paid for me to go on several school trips during the daytime, which I was able to do without my parents even being aware. I knew it was pointless to ask them, for there was always a marathon row, culminating in them telling me I didn't deserve treats, so I just gave up asking.

One such trip was to the Ideal Home Exhibition at which she and I had such a wonderful time that we forgot to rejoin our group at the allocated time. The best part for me was sampling all the mouth-watering foods in the food hall; I was so underweight by this time I was almost emaciated I guess. The message "Will Susan Bonson and Sandra Parrot [not our names but certainly appropriate] come to such-and-such area," boomed out of the Tannoy, jolting us back into reality, as we tore around looking for the designated area. Now over an hour late, the wrath of my teachers was insignificant compared to what Alice and the WW would do in retribution for my having deigned to go on a trip.

Someone up there was on my side, as, although the coach had departed, one of the members of staff who had travelled in her own car for some reason had remained behind to convey us home! We were in detention for a week for which I had to find excuses, and which caused punishment at home too but this was nothing to what being found out would have exposed me.

I hit the same problems when we went to a matinee performance of one of Shakespeare's plays at the Mermaid Theatre. Susie decided, at the commencement of the interval, to conduct a guided sightseeing tour of the area for me and several other adventurous souls, all of whom she ruled magnanimously. I wasn't adventurous any more, of course. I was timid and introverted, but where Susie, my idol, went, I most certainly followed. We slipped out...only when we slipped back, the second act was virtually over, and our teachers had sent out a search party thinking we had been abducted, and all hell broke lose...

There was on this occasion a letter to my parents...which didn't quite make it home and was responded to with a very articulate reply from my father...well, Susie was a marvellous forger as I was to learn on this and many subsequent occasions! Once again the detention resulted in double punishments.

To those who have never experienced violence in their life, it will probably sound an odd thing to say, but the physical violence almost became a way of life to me, an unacceptable and very painful one yet something which, from a child's point of view, just seemed totally, illogically, to be my lot. I couldn't remember a time when my limbs weren't aching, when cuts didn't smart on my body. I accepted bruises, old and new, merging when I wearily took my clothes off, became resigned to a constant headache from the perpetual hair-pulling, head-banging. I didn't seem to have recall of a time when this wasn't happening, just a constant haze of bewilderment and I felt that somehow, I didn't know how, I must be really bad to deserve it. It was not the physical onslaughts that finally wore me down but the constant verbal harassment, the endless innuendo that I was the lowest of the low, not fit to breathe the same air as them. I couldn't bear it any longer and it was driving me to the brink of despair. I was a lost soul.

# —SEVEN—
# THE POINT OF NO RETURN

Occasionally the beatings were so ferocious that I lost consciousness, coming to several hours later—that really frightened me. I had got to the stage when I began to think I was not going to wake up from the aftermath of them. As I rose and faced the trepidation of another day, I always wondered if this was to be my last and whether it would really matter if it was. Night times now were almost as terrifying as the days even though I was in the relative sanctuary of my own room. Daylight or darkness, there was no sunshine in my life any more. Sometimes I used to try and create my own dreams—closing my eyes and imagining myself walking across green meadows, a babbling stream nearby, a happy dog (Waggy of course), frolicking at my side, a gaggle of geese ambling along. Memories of the happy times of my holiday aunt and uncle perhaps, or I'd even recall my very favourite picture that used to hang in my beloved Auntie Ciss and Nell's house entitled *To Pastures New* by Sir James Guthrie. How I longed to be that little girl in the picture, walking along without a care in the world...but that was not for the likes of a bad, wicked person like me and, when I opened my eyes, the reality was always there.

Always with aching heart and pain-wracked body, mentally and physically exhausted, sleep brought me no relief for I would wake in the midst of the most terrible nightmares, where ghouls took my soul to hell. I would be wringing wet, often wetting myself at the sheer terror of it all. Instinctively I knew somehow that I had to fight back if I was to survive. My thirteenth birthday was a turning point for me when for the first time I really questioned why...?

Just after this, in the middle of one such incident, when my head was being banged against the sink taps, I summoned up all of my strength, freed myself and slapped Alice across the face with all my might. I held my breath, waiting for the repercussions—was this it, the end? Anything was preferable to this—but they never came. Alice gasped with the impact—for a little one I must have packed a punch—paused as if in slow motion, then walked away, visibly shocked. From that day onwards, I still got slaps, pushes and pinches, hair-pulling, but never the frenzied attacks by which I felt so threatened and which made me believe that I might not survive.

I never hit her again either; to this day I don't know where I plucked up the courage to do so on this one and only occasion. Alice was only a slight person but when she had the bit between her teeth she had the strength of a dozen men.

Sadly, the verbal abuse never stopped: she looked at and treated me with such contempt and loathing that the only way I got through this living hell was to shut my mind to her and withdraw into my own world.

I lived for my imagination, my inner world; I had an insatiable appetite for the experiences of others for I had none of my own, and wow! According to my school chums, particularly the inimitable Susie, they were some experiences, for they had discovered boys!

I hung on every word, feasting on the chatter of my worldlier peers. Drooling at their boy talk, listening to them giggling at the expense of those gangly youths whom they were fluttering their eyelashes at or giving covert looks in the playground. I was so envious of the lives that they were leading, of how they looked, of their happiness. Certainly no one would have given me a second glance. I was getting taller but pitifully thin. I didn't even wear a bra—I didn't need one but I wouldn't have had the money to buy one even if I did! The nearest I came to boys was a crush on my teacher…Mrs Chandler was her name.

With hindsight of course I realise it was just a desperately lonely child reaching out for attention and affection. I pestered her with poems and letters. I never went outside the house to meet anyone else, but if I had done, by now I was so introverted I would have been terrified even of starting a conversation. I genuinely didn't think anyone would have wanted to have anything to do with me…I was so bad.

To her credit, she and many of the teachers realised that my life was not that of a 'normal' teenager, but without putting a finger on it as to the reason. She treated me with kindness and concern and yes, I was her favourite, in spite of her denials to the more outspoken of my classmates. At school I was more or less under Mrs Chandler's protection and the supreme Susie's of course. I responded to the kindness she showed me with adoration and quality of class work, which exceeded even her expectations.

At school I at least had the knowledge that the very small handful of my peers who allowed me into their circle (most didn't want to know me, this odd apparition in scruffy clothes, frightened of her own shadow) liked me for what I was. Or maybe it was Susie's intervention—she was certainly held in healthy regard within her peer group. I was hopeless at sports, having no co-ordination whatsoever, and so was always the last to be picked for netball and hockey teams, and so on. I used to dread the games lessons, knowing that I would always be the one that neither side wanted, that there would be groans from the unfortunate team who had to have me on board. I lived only for the opportunities to lose myself in books denied me at home, thirsting for knowledge. Devouring other people's lives was my life.

I recorded fantasy happenings in my makeshift diary, stories of boyfriends, exciting escapades, feeding off the lifestyles of my peers (although in likelihood much of what they boasted of was pretence to them too). By now I was fourteen, a sad little figure.

My tormentors continued to treat me as though I was something they had brought in on their feet, and I was barely spoken to. At the very height of my rejection and unhappiness I felt I could go on no longer. I just couldn't face any more and I decided to 'end it all' and join my mum whom I felt would still love me in spite of my being the evil person I obviously was. I reasoned that although she would be in heaven, being so sweet and good in her life, and I would be destined for hell, surely she would find a way to come and see me—anywhere had to be a better place than where I was now.

In the bedrooms were old-fashioned gas-type heaters, which you lit with a match. I went around the entire floor of the house turning them on. I had no reservations, no hesitancy, I just wanted out...

I said a little prayer, asking my mum to help me, then I curled up in bed and went to sleep...

It wasn't a cry for help. After all, there was no one to help me; I just wanted for there to be an end to it all, for the nightmare to be over once and for all.

No one was upstairs, nor were there any smokers in the house until my father returned. As he entered, he must have smelt the gas immediately and rushed upstairs.

I was unconscious. He evacuated the house and my recollection is that when I returned to this world I was cradled in his arms outside in the garden. Whether he had to resuscitate me I have no idea but he was a qualified medic from the war and currently a first-aider so he could have done so.

He was weeping copiously...

They got together in a huddle to decide whether I needed to go to hospital or see a doctor, whispering together in undertones, but they were too frightened to take me. Dad was remonstrating with them—Alice and the WW: 'How could you have been driven her to such despair to do what she's done?'

Half-walking, half-carrying me into the house, what came out of this was my obvious desperate unhappiness. He, of course, knew about it, he couldn't have failed to, but had buried his head in the sand. Now he was bitterly ashamed. I was admonished to tell no one and didn't. I told him I didn't want to live with them any more but there didn't seem to be any options.

Susie came up with one…I could for the time being live with them. Dad apparently spoke with Susie's mum on the phone and she agreed. (Knowing Susie's adeptness at forgery, to this day I don't know if he spoke to her or to Susie, I suspect the latter, but I was in seventh heaven.) I was getting out of this hell on earth; I had turned a chapter in my life even if this was a temporary solution.

Susie's family were so different…Mum was of German origin, a harsh, plain-speaking lady who worked like a Trojan in various jobs to support the household and her hobby, dog racing. Her dad never spoke much at all, watched a bit of telly when he wasn't working and, like her mum, loved racing but seemingly not in the company of his wife. Then there was Uncle C, a rotund, jolly chap who accompanied Susie's mum on all leisure activities like dog racing, dog racing, and dog racing! Her dad seemed to accept this strange situation; Uncle C was part of the family. Then there was Susie and her older brother who was in his early twenties. He was to provide my introduction into other aspects of life that hitherto I had only heard about…but more of that later.

When I turned up on the doorstep, case in hand, Susie simply introduced me to the family, as 'This is Olive, she's coming to stay.'

Mum looked me up and down and said in her very guttural accent, 'There's less meat on her than a skinned rabbit! She's a bag of bones!' which made me think it was the first she'd heard of my coming there.

She didn't say very much more to me then or ever really, but that was her way, and when she did it was always sarcastic and brusque. But in spite of her limitations of speech in my direction, I am convinced that she would, should a need have arisen, and indeed on the occasions when it did, have defended me with her life. I owe her a very great deal.

In this household everyone was busy, busy, busy. Mum cared for herself and Uncle C but no one else. Susie was self-sufficient, looking after herself.

The circumstances transported me back to the days when Louise had just died and I had lived on a diet of cakes and goodies; only this time it was something called Chicklets which I suppose were like fish cakes but of chicken, chips and ice cream. These formed Susie's stable eating habits. Having lived on a very meagre diet for quite a few years, I thought I'd died and gone to heaven!

Susie had ample proportions, now I knew why…the freezer was crammed full of the things. Consuming so many calories for the first time in years you'd have thought I'd have filled out a bit. But no—I still deserved the Olive Oil label.

Susie had no restrictions placed on her time; she came and went as she wanted and we went out and about all over the place; Susie had crushes on all sorts of people— it was another world opening up. Virtually a year older than me, we were chalk and cheese in life's experiences but I tagged along euphorically For the first time in three years I dared let myself take a breath without looking over my shoulder, dared to speak without waiting for the repercussions.

But all too soon it came to an abrupt end. The bombshell fell out of the sky... . There was a phone call.

Apparently Alice or WW had found my fantasy diary in my bedroom at home. In my lonely sad state with nothing but my imagination it had been my escape valve, taken from my peers' stories; it depicted escapades with boys, and sexual adventures—writing such rubbish filled the empty shell that was my life.

Well all the razzmatazz they'd invented about me had nothing on this one!! I was doomed.

I was, according to my very stern father, to return home immediately to face the repercussions! I'd had approximately three months of freedom, of living normally in whatever normal is. I wasn't afraid to speak, to laugh and for the first time in quite a few years a tiny bit of the old Sandra was peeping out from the shutters I had so firmly encased myself to obliterate the rejection and hurt. At last I almost wasn't frightened of my own shadow.

I was blossoming, borrowing Susie's clothes, although I looked like orphan Annie most of the time in them, I didn't care. During this time I had seen Dad once outside of school merely because he had been passing by. Alice I'd not seen at all. It was certainly no loss.

During my stay at Susie's, I had become ill with severe stomach pains, vomiting, and so on. After ignoring me for a few days—and most of the time Susie's mum didn't appear to notice I was there anyway—I think she thought it was probably our diet of Chicklets that we consumed in such huge quantities. When she realised I wasn't getting any better, she frogmarched me to the local GP who sent me to the hospital with a suspected appendicitis.

In all they kept me there for three weeks before whipping my appendix out (there wasn't anything wrong with it, but the pain disappeared from that day!) and apart from signing the mandatory consent forms on my admission for an operation, when he was there for all of five minutes, I hadn't seen hair nor hide of Dad for the whole period.

It was as if (to his relief) I had ceased to exist. He had relinquished all responsibility.

It was Susie and friends who had visited me daily to keep me cheerful, even my schoolteacher idol came by. Now I was to relinquish it all and return home to face the music and it was going to eclipse the Last Night of the Proms and all for what… a lonely child's fantasy world.

No way!

# — EIGHT —
# ROLLER COASTERS

I was totally desperate, not knowing which way to turn. I had told Susie about the conversation with my father—about the diary—but, of course, I was too terrified to tell her the true reasons—the depths of deprivation I was forced to live in at home. I couldn't face it again, I hadn't the strength to fight. At my wits' end, Susie and I decided to run away. Susie did it purely out of camaraderie for me; as an adventure. I had no money but Susie had enough in the post office and here, there and everywhere. We hastily packed and left, leaving a note for Susie's mum.

We boarded the first train to Southend-on-Sea. Why Southend, I've no idea, other than I had read of the marvellous fun fair. It was the first place that came into my head. I had always had a thing about fun fairs (rather like Butlins) possibly because I'd never been to one. I'd always wanted to go on a roller coaster.

Although as a child we'd gone to the seaside for day trips, Auntie Nell always put the block on Auntie Ciss and I venturing in the fairground (although I am sure she would have been as game to go on the roller coaster as I was as she was full of fun). She would issue a categorical 'no!' wagging her finger sternly. You didn't dice with Auntie Nell and Auntie Ciss, and I had a very healthy respect for them! Now we were off on an adventure but I was too petrified even to think about it. That first night we stayed in a bed and breakfast; it was wonderful. If they questioned why two young girls were on their own they never said, but Susie was nearing sixteen and looked older; me, I just looked like a ragamuffin!

We feasted on breakfast, eating them out of house and home, and then spent the day in the fair. Oh what heaven! I lost track of the number of times we went on the waterslide, the roller coaster and the waltzers. Susie fluttered her eyelashes a few times at the youths running the rides and we had quite a few freebies. Unfortunately we rapidly spent all of our money, freebies or not, and the well ran dry.

Undaunted, we wandered up and down on the seafront and the foreshore and made our plans to sleep in one of the bus-type beach shelters. We played silly girlie games with various groups of lads also wandering around, presumably before making their way home after a day at the sea. It was innocent harmless fun.

We watched the illuminations of the seafront dim and extinguish as night came, but unfortunately with it came two police officers in a car that had caught a glimpse of us in the shelter. Instinctively we ran…thinking they were after us for running away, whereas in reality they didn't know who we were from Adam and were just doing their job, showing natural concern at spotting two young girls obviously not at home in their beds.

When they eventually caught up with us, as was inevitable, they asked just one question: 'How old are you?' We saw no reason to lie: 'Fifteen,' accompanied on my part by a flood of tears. 'Oh God,' said one of them, 'why couldn't you be sixteen!!'

We spent the night in a cell at Southend Police Station; at least we had a bed (of sorts) and breakfast.

We were told that 'our parents' were on their way to collect us. I still had the saga of 'the diary' hanging over me and so was terrified witless. Susie was nonchalant, more concerned about the likelihood of us being split up and my not living there any more... I hadn't thought of that one so was even more distraught. Susie's mum arrived, driven by Uncle C to collect her but not me, as I had prayed would be the case. She told me my father was on the way...told us we were a pair of silly cows...and *he* was as mad as mad could be.

The police had asked about the lads they had spotted in our vicinity but seemed satisfied by the honest explanation that they had just been following us around. By the time my father arrived I really wished I were dead. However his initial reaction (playing to an audience) was that of resigned humour: 'After all, I ran away when I was a boy. Girls will be girls!'

Alone together for a moment, I launched into an explanation of why I had felt I needed to do this, the fictitious nature of my diary and so on. He listened without speaking.

My expectations that he would trust my explanations (as indeed Susie's mum had and they were now on the way back home) were short-lived...my father asked, using the fact that there had been boys in the vicinity when we were spotted as an excuse, that I be checked by a police surgeon that I hadn't been sexually assaulted or, as was really in his mind, whether I was or wasn't a virgin!

His articulate request, which he made seem very plausible, given his way with words, was agreed to. I don't know of course in his brief chat with the police officers out of my presence whether he had offered any other information to them, but no one asked how I felt about this. I was subjected to the indignity of my feet being hung in stirrups whilst a police doctor (albeit a very kindly one) checked whether my hymen was intact.

At the last moment my father remembered my bicycle accident on the Great West Road and interjected that, if there were any problems, they could possibly be attributed to this. There weren't any problems of course, I was sexually totally inexperienced. I'd never been in the vicinity of a boy/man, even less intimate with one: who in their right mind would have been interested in me anyway? He subjected me to this ordeal, which was quite terrifying, without any concern or compassion for me at all. Everything that had happened over the past few months was pushed to the back of his mind as he strove to satisfy his own mind.

His fears allayed, he decided we should call in at his sisters, Auntie Gladys in her B & B (you remember, the one who washed her smalls in the pot water!!) before driving home or, as he put it, putting off the evil moment of deciding what to do with me.

In spite of his having turned his back on me while burying his head in the sand as to the problems and unhappiness I suffered at home, with childlike illogic I had, until that moment in the police station, loved my father with doglike devotion. Although he had been a party to the anguish I went through, somehow I had always thought it wasn't his fault, that in a way he too was a 'victim'. However, the indignity he had insisted I be put through, his failure to believe my story (and yet I had never knowingly lied to him—not told him about things, yes, like school outings, but never in confrontation told him an untruth) was a turning point and I told him I would not return to live in that house again. I would run away—again and again, if I was forced to.

I think for him too this may have been a turning point, the crucial moment when the façade of normality had been well and truly lifted. He mumbled excuses about how unhappy *he* was within his marriage, that *he* had only married to give me a mother and yes, for *his* survival—perhaps it was better if I didn't live with them any more.

I wanted to scream at him that *he* had failed *me*, ruined my life, and stood by, doing nothing as I was transformed from a happy, loving, gregarious child into a terrified, inhibited, nervous teenager. The words were there: my brain was bursting with anger and frustration but they were never uttered.

# —NINE—
# NORMALITY

He took me back to Susie's, talked to her mum, put everything on a business footing i.e. money for board, and so on. I waited, almost holding my breath to see if she would agree. It was the only time I heard her speak a kind word, well of sorts! 'Poor cow, she's frightened of her own shadow, she can stay with our Susie.' Words from heaven! Apart from that occasion when money did change hands, I honestly don't think he ever sent another penny and she kept me out of goodness or possibly pity; either way I owe her a great debt of gratitude. He discharged his responsibilities from that moment on.

Susie and I continued to live our eccentric lifestyle. Big changes for Susie: she had left school and was working at London Airport for, as was then, BEA, as an office junior.

Susie had for over a year had a crush on a coach driver she had met on a school trip and chatted up. He was old enough to be her grandfather (well almost!) and had nothing about him that was remotely reminiscent of the posters she displayed everywhere of good-looking pop stars or the crushes she'd had on delicious young men who had crossed her path in the past. In fact he was very ordinary. But she was steadfast in her devotion. Every evening she met up with him, sometimes in his coach, or in his car, and I tagged along, usually lost in daydreams whilst they did whatever it was they were doing...

If I knew and of course I did, I didn't want to know. On occasions he brought along a pal with him, probably prompted by Susie as company for me. Thus the first man I ever came into contact with was called Ted—a sort of Tom Jones look-alike (if the lights were dim or in total blackout!) probably forty-something. We sat in the coach and had a bit of a kiss and a cuddle until he undid his fly and pushed into my hand something that resembled a slimy, very large cucumber with appendages attached to the ends, covered in black gorilla-like hair. A Tom Jones look-alike you will recall I said, but here I must hasten to add that this is based purely on assumption. I haven't, very unfortunately on my part, seen Tom Jones' private parts!

I catapulted from that seat quicker than the speed of light. Poor guy! However, he probably had a lucky escape, given my total lack of dexterity, not to mention sexual experience. I would probably have squeezed it to death, depriving him of his manhood forever.

As I said before, of course I knew Susie was having sex but we never talked about it, surprisingly really, because we shared a bedroom and nattered into the small hours most of the time. For me she was like the sister I had never had. But, although we talked about these things in general terms, what was happening in our lives personally seemed to be taboo. Just as I didn't talk about the bleaker side of my life with Alice, she didn't mention her escapades with her coach-driver friend.

It came doubly as a shock then that one evening Susie's dad was already out and her mum and Uncle C were preparing to go for their soiree at the dog track, when her mum summoned me into the living room. She pointed to a large enamel bowl on the floor full of boiling water, with a large bar of red carbolic soap and a weird black pump-like object floating in it, telling me in her brusque guttural accent, that Susie was 'up the duff' and that I was to help her. Susie would tell me what to do… . Then, as if she had asked me to vacuum the carpet, she swept out for her evening's entertainment.

Susie was ensconced miserably in the chair. She had no idea what to do and even if she had I was incapable of carrying it out. She'd have probably landed up with a punctured bowel or something. I carried the bowl through to the kitchen and left it, the soap bar congealing and the smell of carbolic pervading the room. We waited in miserable apprehension for Susie's mum to reappear, me in trepidation because it was the first time I'd crossed her, so to speak. Taking the coward's way out I went to bed, waiting in the darkness for Susie to join me but falling asleep before she did.

It wasn't mentioned again. Susie was taken to see a lady that her mum knew of, although I didn't know anything about it until after the event, returned to my care. I was told to look after her and keep her quiet.

I have no wish to linger over this most awful time. Here we were, two young girls: I did my best to comfort and cuddle her, and under my instructions trying not to let the rest of the house hear her cries, and there were plenty, through that seemingly never-ending night.

She eventually evacuated the source of all of the pain and exhaustively slept. I cleaned up the ravages as best I could before, like Susie, falling into an exhausted sleep. Susie was sixteen; I was in my first half of my fifteenth year. The memory of this has remained with me always.

Susie continued her relationship with her coach-driver friend. I spent less and less time out with them, correctly feeling in the way.

My own unwilling induction into the delights (as opposed to, as conceived by me, horrors) of sexual activity (following Susie's abortion!) were about to commence but I didn't need to go outside to look for it, it was under my roof.

Susie had a brother whom by then was in his mid-twenties. He seemed to be an elusive figure, out most of the time either working or playing and, as this wasn't the sort of household with communal mealtimes, I hardly ever saw him.

He saw me however.

By this time, I suppose unconsciously on my part, I had developed from less of the gangly child into a young lady. Still like a beanpole, or tall and willowy as certain magazines may depict, I still had very little to offer in the curves department but my features had developed into those of a young woman. It was ironic really, for the first time in many years, in this house I had felt safe—not loved, it wasn't that sort of household, but secure that my space was my own where I could relax without awaiting with sure-fire certainty for the onslaught that would sooner rather than later be coming my way!

Now this newfound security was coming under threat in another way. J (Susie's brother) homed in on me at every opportunity, always taking care that it was not in sight of either his mum or Susie (both of whom in varying degrees he had a healthy respect for and wasn't about to rock the boat). He used varying tactics to persuade me to go along with his advances, not least that he would tell his mother that I had given him the 'come-on' and she would boot me out of the house if I didn't do as he asked.

He of course, I don't think, had the slightest idea of the terror that prospect would invoke (unless Susie or her mum had spoken of it, which I doubt since even Susie my very closest confidante never really knew it all). Why? Because ultimately, on my part, and no matter how ill-conceived this actually was, there was still this loyalty thing to my family and I didn't want other people to know how bad they were; and perhaps, to an even greater extent, there was the idea—ever present in the back of mind—that I was to blame for everything that had befallen me.

At every opportunity we indulged in petting but fell short of intercourse. I think that the knowledge that I wasn't a willing participator was its own contraception. Ironically, if he had shown me any affection instead of coercing me, I would have been more than willing, so desperately did I want someone to love me whom I in return could love.

Whilst he didn't take my virginity, ironically someone else did for probably just that very reason mentioned in the last paragraph—that sheer desperation to be loved and give love. I was persuaded by Susie to accompany her and her coach-driver friend out one evening as they had arranged a date for me. Evenings out with them both were a very infrequent occurrence these days as I always felt in the way and felt she deserved her privacy.

His name was Alan and he did something at London Airport. It was a steady and important job. Susie told me with a giggle that he 'walks with a lisp', and he certainly walked with an ungainly action. He was shy and quiet, mid-twenties, not the stuff dreams were made of, and he seemed to be as much a fish out of water as I was.

We drove around aimlessly, landing up at, of all places, Mortlake Cemetery. Alan and I left the car for a stroll to give the others some privacy. It was freezing cold and we light-heartedly had a cuddle, more to keep warm than because passion was rearing its head, but in my newfound worldliness I obviously gave out signals that took us both to the point of no return.

It was over in minutes—no fireworks, fanfares; it all seemed rather undignified (although thinking about it, it probably was, leaning up against a tombstone!)

And, rather embarrassed, we made our way back to the car.

I continued meeting up with Alan on the infrequent occasions I went out with Susie. He didn't make my heart beat faster but I suppose there were worse ways of killing time. I'm sure he felt the same way, if he thought anything much of me he didn't convey it but then he wasn't a young man of words.

Unfortunately a thunderbolt struck. To this day I have no idea of what his source was. My father turned up at the house breathing fire and brimstone!

(In the few months I had been at Susie's I had not seen him at all, he had never visited, or got in touch and he certainly hadn't sent Susie's mum any money for my keep. There had been a time when I had needed to collect some of my belonging and school things. With trepidation and with Susie to hold my hand, I made sure it would be when he was at home for my protection. Kept in the front hall, denied access to what had been my bedroom, I had been met with a very frosty response and a stark awareness that no one in the house, himself included, had any sort of a welcome to offer me. I was clearly an unwelcome visitor and it was certainly out of sight out of mind.)

Now here he was, levelling some very nasty accusations at Susie's mother, which boiled down to the fact that 'it has been brought to my notice', that she was allowing her son to gain carnal knowledge of me!

To the very best of my knowledge Susie's mum was completely in the dark as to the relationship between J and myself, as indeed was Susie, judging by her astonished look.

Susie's mum was not a person to be crossed lightly even if my father did have the upper hand with his more eloquent use of the English language, dire threats of police intervention, and general outrage. Not surprisingly my bags were swiftly packed and I left that house which, as eccentric as it was, had been such a happy, and probably more to the point, safe haven for me.

## —TEN—
## SANCTUARY

He had nowhere to take me, had not thought about the consequences of his actions until the moment we got into his car. He had no option other than to take me home.

We didn't talk in the car except for a few ominous words that set my heart racing and let that old familiar knot of fear well up in my stomach.

'Alice is not happy!'

Even then I was ill-prepared for the sheer hatred that greeted me when his key turned in the lock. Alice had worked herself up into a complete frenzy at the thought of my returning to her territory. She was completely beyond control and I knew with sickening intuitiveness that if I remained in that house for even one night it would in all likelihood, be my last!

My father, in his usual inimitable style, had feigned a business meeting, and so turned tail and disappeared, leaving me to it.

I stood frozen to the spot on the doorstep and Alice advanced menacingly towards me...

I turned tail also and walked out into the darkness, not knowing where I was going but that it had to be preferable to setting foot over the threshold of that house.

I walked for miles, not knowing or caring about destination, my school uniform the only protection against the elements. I do remember it was a bitterly cold night. Someone kindly stopped and offered me a lift. They were they said going to Hammersmith. I accepted but have no recollection of the conversation we had or how I fended off their obvious curiosity as to why I was out alone walking.

I watched the people happily, noisily leaving the Hammersmith Palais, enjoying the company of their peers without a care in the world.

I watched as the streets quietened and traffic dwindled almost to nothing. No one had noticed me slouched against a wall or if they had, they were too busy wrapped up in their own lives. I didn't know what I was going to do other than that I was never ever going to return to that house.

I had borne the burden of my tormenter's abuse in my inner soul for just too long and anything, no matter how awful, was preferable to facing it again.

It was raining heavily and I huddled, shivering against the wall trying to get some protection from the elements, the streets deserted, the occasional car careering through the puddles on the roads, oblivious to me.

Once again the peacefulness of the night was shattered by the arrival of a passing police car and for the second time in my short life I spent the remainder of that awful night in a police cell, this time in Hammersmith Police Station.

There was more graffiti on the walls than in Southend and a lot more noise but here in this anonymous, disinfectant-smelling (masking the smell of urine and vomit) anti-social environment I felt safe, secure in the knowledge that this was to be a turning point for me and that I would never again be subjected to the hurt, rejection and abuse that had featured thus far in my life.

Come morning, I drew from my inner strength and told all. I was asked if there was anyone I wanted to help me through this and illogically I could think of no one.

I felt totally alone but strangely happy that I would no longer have to shoulder the burden. I told my story and repeated it again and yet again, this time in the company of social workers.

I went from the police station to a children's home in Willesden. Here lived a small group of children all much younger than me and I spent the short duration of my stay there playing the little mother in much the same way as I had always longed to do with my sister and brother, except I had never dared.

I had a welfare officer. Her name was Miss Willett and she was a kindly older lady who did her utmost to make my stay and impending court appearance as relaxing as possible. I had no contact with Dad nor, if I am honest, did I want any.

At Susie's I had rapidly had to make the transition into an adult without complaint because of the way of life we led. It was my exit from purgatory. Now, I was able, albeit temporarily, to revert to seeing things through the eyes of a child again with my young companions.

So I went to court—in need of care and protection I believe the terminology was then.

I waited quietly whilst the chapters of the past few years of my life were opened, dissected and discussed. Nothing was spared. Dad was there but I have no recall of what he replied in response to the questions that were asked of him, other than that he was full of contrition and remorse…or was he? Was this once again an accomplished performance for the benefits of those accusing him (or me)? I didn't really know, I was too weary of it all to care.

I answered the questions that were asked of me, summoning up a bravery that I didn't know I had.

Many of the people in the court, hardened as they were in all probability to situations like mine, were in tears as they listened to my story. I was placed in the care of the local authority and returned temporarily to Willesden.

Not that I ever think there was, but had there ever been a minute shred of hope (and there's always hope isn't there, in the very deepest compartment of your heart?) that Alice would ever come to accept me, it was shattered by the press coverage of my visit to the juvenile court.

Whilst, of course, no names were mentioned at all—just a brief, factual report of the hearing—the headline of the small piece glared out: 'Girl More Sinned Against than Sinned, Wicked Stepmother Blamed'.

# ELEVEN

# SECURITY

My time at the children's home went very quickly. I don't have much recollection other than being looked after by kindly people and in turn looking after the smaller children who vied for my attention—something I could have handled all day.

I did get to know my welfare officer well though, and to trust and respect her. I learnt through her that my father and Alice had moved to Kent presumably with WW in tow.

Dad himself had not been in touch since the court case, not even to let me know they had moved.

There were some monumental changes to come at this time. Without the support of Miss Willett (my welfare officer) I would never have coped. She nurtured me, building my confidence, helping me to build my self-esteem, all of which had taken a nose dive since I left Susie's. I had to move. I was just too old for the children's home, the children were all much younger than me and Miss

Willett explained it had only been a transitional emergency arrangement, but I could have happily stayed there and was very apprehensive at the prospect of change. With bag and baggage (though not a lot of that), despite being taken out and bought the necessities by the home (and Miss Willet had braved the lion's den, so to speak, to collect some of my stuff), we went to what was to be my new home, a hostel situated in Shepherds Hill in Highgate.

The front door was opened at our ring by someone undressed, towel around her hair, clearly expecting the visitor to be for her. Upon realising that this wasn't the case, she turned on her heel, leaving us on the doorstep. The place was mayhem; someone was screaming abuse in the background. Transported back to my days with Alice, I froze on the spot and had to be propelled in by the gentle but insistent arm of Miss Willett. The person in charge was courteous but reminded me a bit of what I would have expected a prison warden to be. I don't think she would have stood any nonsense from anyone and could clearly take care of herself—this in marked contrast to the gentle house parents at the children's home. Hindsight would show me that such qualities would be necessary for the job in Shepherds Hill. The staff certainly had their work cut out. My room was to be a sort of mini dormitory shared by three other girls. I was petrified at the prospect. I sat on the bed which was to be mine, wishing the floor would open me up. Miss Willett had left, promising to be in touch in a couple of days. I felt she had deserted me at the entrance to the Lion's Den. Those whom were at home wasted no time in getting to see 'the new girl'. By their conversation I quickly realised that many of them had been placed in the care of the courts for misdemeanours rather than being in need of care like myself. They were tough cookies! I think the house was home to about twelve or so girls. Having ascertained that I posed no threat to their boyfriends, nor was any challenge to the pecking order in the house, they realised I wasn't really worth the time of day. They were worldly and streetwise, far more worried about current boyfriends and how to overcome the 'Coming In' curfew than by this particular room mate.

There followed a couple of days of inquisitive nit-picking, making fun and imitating my 'posh' voice, after which I think they gave up on me as a bad job. I wasn't adept at shop lifting, had no gory details of love affairs to impart, hadn't seen the latest film, couldn't dance, hadn't any luxury underwear or clothes worth nicking (in fact even if I had, they wouldn't have fitted any of their voluptuous figures anyway as I was still in a size 32AA cup bra!) In fact, overall, I was a dead loss! My only use, it would seem, would be to do the odd chore for them—a bit of washing, open the occasional window to let them in! They didn't bully, but for someone like me, frightened of her own shadow, they certainly intimidated. I was so eager to be liked, frightened of aggression, so compliant that I willingly undertook everyone's jobs on the rota. They had a really easy ride but I wasn't complaining and I certainly wouldn't have had the confidence to stand up for myself and say no. I washed and ironed, cleaned and carried out the lists of chores for just about everyone in the hostel.

I remain forever grateful to the houseparent, however, who intuitively realised how completely out of my depth I was (or maybe it was the gentle persuasion of Miss Willett, for I certainly wouldn't have put it past her) and moved me into a tiny little room of my own. I think it had been the linen cupboard before, so miniscule was it, with no window, but it was all mine and I could shut the door and lose myself in a book, oblivious to my surroundings and the noisy goings-on of those around me.

The second major change at this time was that I went out to work. After lots of discussion with Miss Willett as to the possibilities of going to a new school or to college, which, although I was as bright as a button, we mutually decided my confidence just wasn't up to, I had decided that I would like to do my nursing training. At barely sixteen, I was not yet old enough. The viable option was that I did a pre-nursing cadet course. This entailed working in various departments of the hospital such as X-Ray, Outpatients, Physiotherapy as well as attending college for a couple of days a week. It was a huge step for me, as I was so lacking in confidence. Who would want me? But, propelled and supported by the inimitable Miss Willett, to my utter amazement I was accepted but had to wait for the next intake. In the meanwhile, via an agency, again arranged by Miss Willett, I managed to get a job as a very office junior in a promotions company situated in Soho Square in London.

If it hadn't been for the support and commitment of Miss Willett, nurturing me, helping me build myself from a zero self-esteem and look forward to a future, I have no doubt I would have just given up. So great was this exceptional lady towards me that she even took me to her home (well hers and half a dozen cats and dogs), a tiny little bungalow in Chipperfield in Hertfordshire, to share her weekend leisure on several memorable occasions. If anyone was instrumental in helping to heal the wounds I carried so deeply it was she. I owed her so much.

She became a sort of surrogate aunt; and, talking of aunts, she came with me to visit Louise's sisters, all a little older, a little sadder, but, without exception, warmly welcoming to me. My Auntie Gwen (probably acquainted with my limited clothes situation by Miss Willett although not within my earshot) took me out to buy some material and dress patterns and my Auntie Nell set to work with her knitting needles to knit me a couple of cardigans to go with them so that I could at least make my work debut with some clothes on my back!

You can never turn back the clock and things would never be quite the same as in the happy years with them preceding Louise's death, but at least I had rekindled my contact with them and they would now always remain my family.

I led a very insular lifestyle. I became quite adept at walking the mile or so to the station in Highgate and going on the tube to London and making my way to Soho Square where I immersed myself in mountains of filing, tea-making and typing. (Fortunately typing had been something I had studied at school.) I would often not speak to anyone other than asking if they wanted sugar in their coffee or tea. This was an exceedingly busy building, hustle and bustle all of the time, but I just merged into the background and nobody really noticed me for which I was grateful.

My only claim to fame was that I once shared a sandwich with Jo Brown (he was one of the stars this agency managed), and I think that was because he was starving and didn't know where the nearest coffee bar was and there was no one else there at the time to ask, and not for a moment because he wanted to share half an hour with me.

I bet he forgot about it a long while before I did. There were beautiful people flitting around in and out of offices all of the time but not in the circles that I, a lowly junior moved in!

Come time to go home, I'd suffer the ravages of the tube again, sneak into the sanctuary of my little room, and eat something erratically in it, as I couldn't face the mayhem of the communal kitchen; then I would immerse myself in books until bedtime.

I could go where I wanted within the confines of curfew, do what I wanted, eat what I wanted—the reality of that takes a long while to sink in.

I saw Susie sometimes although she had moved in with her coach-driver friend. He always drove her over which made it awkward, so we never had time for a girlie chat like the old days.

I occasionally saw Alan; he now had bought himself an MGA sports car, which did marvels for my street credibility at the hostel when he collected me or dropped me off. We used to go out for a coffee, sometimes a meal. He, like me, was lonely, was shy and didn't really have any social life as such. I think, in kindness, he felt sorry for me, but it wasn't a hearts and flowers relationship on either side.

In the main, however, I did virtually nothing in the time I wasn't at work other than read in my little closet!

I started work at the hospital—the Prince of Wales in Tottenham. Like a clockwork doll, inanimate until someone winds her up, this was 'me'. I loved it! With a thirst for all the knowledge available to me, I became a valued member of a team, treated as an individual, laughed and joked with, not at. Slowly but surely, my confidence resurfaced and I blossomed.

My life at the hostel was still uneventful. I had very little money to spend once I had paid my board; the pay at the hospital was obviously very little. Sometimes, just to break up the hours, I wandered down to the little precinct of shops nearby to buy a bar of chocolate or a magazine. A Greek Cypriot family owned the newsagents. Quietly welcoming, I found that with my newfound confidence I often stayed and chatted, whiling away a couple of hours.

Husband and wife with two or three smallish children, Grandma lived with them and seemingly quite a few other extended family members drifted in and out. They were a traditional Cypriot family, loving and loyal to each other.

If they sensed how lonely I was they didn't say but slowly as I got to know them better, they extended the hand of friendship and I often shared a meal with them, repaying them by working in the shop whilst they put the children to bed and so on. I began to think the world of them and they treated me as one of the family.

Unfortunately, through one of those inexplicable twists of fate, had things been different I could so easily have been a real part of their family.

I mentioned other relatives dashing in and out; several of them were young men who were brothers or nephews of my friends. They lived independently but always maintained a room with the family as well, where they spent occasional nights, probably when they were tapping their brother for money (which was almost always).

A typical Cypriot family, they were tremendously supportive towards these young people as they furthered their careers and sponsored them financially at great hardship to themselves, to help them get a good start in life and their feet on the ladder of success.

One such a person was Kip. He was the brother of my friends, training to be a barrister, the most gorgeous looking man I had ever seen and I fell immediately head over heels in love with him.

Like the rest of the young men in the family he had a flat which he shared with another brother and a couple of cousins as well as coming to the shop one or two nights a week and sleeping over. He paid me attention (as he paid attention to anything reasonably young, or even not so young, of the female gender), flirting with me with his dark beautiful eyes, enormous lashes and exquisite smile and I was 'lost' forever.

We made love at every opportunity at his flat, even in the rooms upstairs above the shop. (I had such a relationship of trust with my friends that they thought nothing was untoward in my going upstairs with Kip to listen to music.)

It was nothing but sex on his part…the virility of a young man in his prime chasing everything in sight. He often let me down, didn't show up and we never did anything but make love and I use that term loosely—on my part it was complete adoration, as I would have gone to the ends of the earth for him had he asked me; on his part, he was just satisfying his healthy appetites and if it wasn't me it would have been someone else he used his charms on.

There was a constant procession of young ladies in and out of the flat for they were all 'at it' at every opportunity. Kip even suggested I might like to get to know his flatmates better…in so little esteem did he place me. I was mortified but would have done so if it meant pleasing him. Fortunately it never came to that. Of course I used to fantasise that he would one day really love me.

The one definite provision on Kip's side of our relationship was that his brother and family, my friends at the shop, should not have any inkling of what was going on. To them he was still their little brother and he milked that to the hilt, always taking money off them and giving out the aura of supreme innocence, dedication to his course work and the law practice he was assigned to. I knew the reality to be very different…it was all play and very little work. He wrapped them round his little finger.

It's funny really, being in love meant, I think (at least that's the explanation I placed on it), that suddenly other men were taking notice of me. I had, with my newfound confidence, allowed others I worked with to persuade me to go to several parties at the nurses' home, lending me clothes, and was astonished that men were paying me attention, flirting with me, finding me attractive, even young doctors who were on such a high pedestal in comparison with me and my lowly duties. I was astounded…but I had no interest in anyone or anything except Kip. He was my reason for living.

# —TWELVE—
# BOMBSHELLS

My love of my work duties, my newborn confidence, the realisation that people around me wanted to be more than a work associate, liking me for who I was, my adoration of Kip meant that I was on cloud nine and several months went by before the reality sank in—that I hadn't had a period for quite a while…

Whilst I was now, I suppose, deemed sexually experienced, I was still in truth very naive and I certainly hadn't practised any form of birth control. On the very rare occasions Alan and I had met up he had always used something and I suppose I had made an assumption that Kip had too. Of course with hindsight I should have appreciated he was far too egotistical to detract from his pleasure in even the minutest way but at the time it didn't even occur to me. Now I began to think the unthinkable—that I might be pregnant.

I told Kip.

I went round to his flat with heavy heart. Ringing the

doorbell, my hands were shaking, reminiscent of the prelude to the physical onslaughts I had suffered at the hands of Alice. My heart was racing.

He opened the door, towel slung casually around his waist, having just emerged from the shower. He was so beautiful and I loved him so much it hurt. Could he possibly, just possibly, find it in his heart to love me and his baby?

'You timed that well, Sandie,' he said, reaching for me as he kicked the door shut with his foot, the towel falling to the ground, oblivious of or not caring that there were others in the flat, his arousal plain for all to see. He propelled me into the bedroom. There was no social niceties, he didn't even give me a chance to take off my coat, no foreplay, just sex. I wanted to say, I need to talk to you…but I was lost.

Afterwards in those moments of togetherness which are traditional to lovers everywhere, or so I imagined and that I longed for so much in my relationship with Kip, I told him—just those two little words: 'I'm pregnant.'

If I had harboured any illusions in my heart of hearts that he had any depth of feeling for me, which of course I wanted so desperately to be the case, they were shattered once and for all in the harsh reality of the moment and the fury he unleashed in my direction.

His anger was terrifying: with an intake of breath, he hit me in one movement which sent me sprawling from the bed to the other side of the room, calling me words that even living in a hostel of streetwise girls, I had never heard before. 'You fucking stupid bitch' was the nicest part. A torrent of abuse still pouring from his mouth he told me, 'I'll arrange to get rid of it. Do anything to wreck my life and you'll be dead.'

Not for one moment did he show me a glimmer of concern or respect, just hatred. Gesturing at the door, he yelled, 'Get out whilst you still can. I'll be in touch in a couple of days. Tell anyone and I'll kill you.' Surely, words of anger, of fear on his part, but no less terrifying to me.

I was outside the flat, my illusions, the fantasy that I had chosen to weave around myself, my feelings for Kip which were so deep they were like a knife cutting away at my heart, all lay in tatters, everything in my life destroyed in minutes. I had given him my love so unconditionally, daring to hope that he might just one day reciprocate. I had allowed him to penetrate the veneer that I had woven around myself to try and shut out the rejection and hurt that had been my life. For a short while he had been 'my world'. Now this too had ended.

I had only had my sixteenth birthday a month or so before. I hadn't celebrated, no one knew, there weren't any cards, never mind presents (but I'd been used to that for years). It hadn't mattered. For the first time in such a lot of years I had been quietly optimistic that the tide was turning for me, that things, just a tweeny bit, were going my way!

And now this!

I was terrified; I had no one to talk to, to confide in about such a sensitive subject. I wouldn't have dared to talk to Miss Willett about it, fearing her wrath. More to the point, I feared her rejecting me, for I valued our relationship so much, and of course I had no family to turn to.

Talking of family, I had seen Dad only once in those months and the only time he had phoned me was to arrange a meeting. I had begun to think he didn't know the hostel telephone number and my address but Miss Willett had rather sadly assured me that he did know both. We met up in London. He had been on a course and we had met up at the station typically, under the clock, prior to him returning home.

He was ill at ease, giving out some small talk but nothing more. He professed to be concerned that I was wondering around on a bitterly cold day in a thin raincoat. I didn't have a winter coat and certainly not the money to buy one. I explained this to him and in his usual flamboyant style he said that he would open a bank account for me and put an amount of money in it every month to enable me to buy necessities like clothes and nursing books when I needed them.

For a brief moment, a warmth spread through me that he did care, did love me, but then I remembered the façade he always needed to present, so I didn't hold my breath. True enough, he did open an account, placed £5 in it but that was the first and last time. Our time together was all of fifteen minutes and he boarded his train without even a backward glance, a kiss or even a hug. It was almost as if I was an acquaintance he had just met. I definitely had no family…

Now with the reality of what was happening to me, everything I had so painstakingly rebuilt in my life crumbled around me and I was no longer the master of my own destiny. I was a terrified child again.

I didn't dare allow myself to even think of this new life that was being nurtured inside me.

I just shut my mind completely to it—it wasn't happening. I was completely cowed by Kip, and there was no hint of the charisma and kindness I had fallen in love with.

He offered me no choices, only curt commands; paranoid that his family would find out, he said he would 'kill me' if they did. I'm sure they were just the words of anger and, yes, of fear on his part, the 'big' man being really a frightened small boy at heart, but so literally did I take his threats that I was frightened even to go near my friends at the shop just in case I let my secret drop out.

Through his medical school contacts, Kip produced some pills, which I was to take to get rid of it. I took them but nothing happened. Kip refused to believe that I had taken them and produced a further dose, which I had to take in front of him. I did as I was told.

Nothing.

He then phoned me at the hostel and demanded that I go around to the flat. When I did so, I found one of his cousins, a medical student, together with his current nurse girlfriend that I had never even met before, with a similar sort of douche apparatus to that which Susie's mum had produced for me to use on her. The memories came flooding back.

Terrified, I allowed them to ravage my body with this evil-smelling concoction. Kip wasn't even there. Then I was admonished to go home and wait and to tell no one, that if anything went 'wrong' to go to the hospital.

Back in my little cubby hole, waiting for the pains and eventual evacuation that had occurred for Susie, waiting and waiting, the hours passed slowly. But they never came…

# –THIRTEEN–
# DESPERATION

These were some of my blackest hours; I didn't eat, I didn't sleep; where could I turn?

I sat in my anonymous little room; no one knew I was there. There seemed to be nowhere for me to go. I felt at that lowest edge when suicide again seemed my only way out. I sat for an entire day at Highgate Station trying to pluck up the courage each time a train came to step out. I must have alerted the attention of the station staff as, in the end, they came to me asking if everything was all right. I wanted to scream, 'No, it isn't,' but I mumbled something unintelligible and went out, stopping to buy lots of aspirins on the way back to my little room.

Inside, I tried to take them. Ironically, I have never in my life been able to swallow a tablet, always gagging and often sick: this was no exception and try as I might I couldn't get those tablets down. Time and time again I tried, I must have only managed to swallow about nine or ten, when I was sick all over the floor. When I had been a little girl my mum had always crushed tablets for me, putting them in a spoonful of jam, tenderly helping me to take them…that seemed a lifetime away now…. In the darkness (I had not put the light on because I didn't want anyone to know I was there, to find me) I choked again and again on these tablets, seeming to me to be the size of tennis balls as I thrust them into my mouth, gulping great swigs of water to try and get them down, tears streaming down my face.

I couldn't even manage to do this properly; I was a failure, it seemed, to me, in everything. In abject misery I sat in the darkness of that little room, for how many hours I just don't know, oblivious to everything, in the very pits of despair.

# FOURTEEN
# THE LIGHT

Someone helped me through these bleakest hours and helped me to turn a corner and showed me a light at the end of the tunnel. I think it was probably the memory of my mother Louise and how much she had loved and cherished me. Now I too had a life growing within me, that had refused to become separated from me, had fought to continue to exist in spite of everyone's efforts and my own acquiescence to their administerings.

Now this was another day and I was determined to fight and find a way; I didn't know how or where, but I knew resolutely that somehow I would bring this new life, this very part of me, into this world and to love and to cherish him or her with my life, my love, with every fibre of my being for the rest of my life.

And thus I turned another chapter of my life.

## —FIFTEEN—
## SURVIVAL

I lied to Kip; it was easy to say that I had lost the baby. He was euphoric and even misguided enough to think we would resume our relationship as before.

Whatever experiences this new situation in my life was going to bring me, an old head sat on young shoulders. With a moment of fleeting sadness (albeit short-lived) I told him I was moving away; he even asked me if I had any friends at the hostel I could introduce to him! Talk about a morale booster!

What gave me even more sadness, however, was that I no longer had the friendship of my shopkeeper friends, having to tell them the same story. Ironically they were the aunts and uncles of this new life developing inside me and I couldn't have wished for kinder and better. They, like me, were sad that I was going away, gave me lots of hugs and asked me to write, but of course I knew that I couldn't.

Alan turned up unexpectedly to see me. I hadn't seen him for ages. He had been working in the south of the country and I had spent an enjoyable weekend with him a while back, exploring the New Forest, but more as friends than anything else.

We didn't keep in touch from one month to the next; it really wasn't that sort or relationship.

I told him I was pregnant. It came out on the spur of the moment. It was completely unplanned on my part and certainly unpremeditated. Maybe again, if you believe in destiny, someone was showing me the light through the tunnel, who knows?

Appearing somewhat bemused, he never once asked me if the child was his so I never had to lie to him (I don't think I could have done). He made the assumption that it was. Maybe in his heart of hearts he wanted it to be, as he was a lonely very introverted person. In real terms, given that I had only seen him once in months, had he looked at the time span involved, he would have realised that it couldn't possibly be the case, but he never did and, maybe deep down, he wanted something that belonged to him too, and was not therefore looking too deeply, who knows?

Anyway he made it so easy. He didn't ask, I didn't lie!

He asked me what I wanted to do and said he would pay for an abortion if that was my choice but I replied that I was going to keep the baby but that, in any case, as I was then some four and a half months pregnant, it was too late.

In real terms, however, had I only been four and a half days, nothing but nothing was going to take my baby away from me now that I had made that decision.

He suggested we get married; very tentatively I have to say, as he wasn't a very positive person and it was at this stage I told him the only lie that I ever needed to. He asked me if I loved him and I said yes.

It was a small price to pay for a tiger to protect her cub…'like' yes, but 'love' no. However, I was certainly committed enough to give it everything I'd got to repay him for being my salvation.

And from liking and respecting someone, love can surely grow? I would certainly give it my best shot to make him glad that he had shown me the way through and do my utmost to make him glad we were sharing his life.

Definitely he didn't love me. Our relationship was not that intense but he had gone through some traumatic times, I believe, in a past relationship; and didn't really want commitment. Yet he was an honourable and kindly man and wanted to do what he considered the right thing by me.

We decided we would get married as soon as possible.

I was of course only sixteen, so a consent form had to be signed, I thought, by a parent.

I rang Dad and told him. The silence was ominous.

Alan and I met up with Dad at Euston Railway Station where he immediately embarked upon a lecture to Alan that he would have to keep me in the way I was accustomed, how disappointed he was, et cetera, I was set to go far…what a waste of my life… . Alan was quite bemused by the whole thing.

Still the same old Dad, presenting the façade for the benefit of an audience, trying to impress! He signed the form, no doubt with a sigh of relief that I was 'off his hands' forever!

Ironically, of course, I was off his hands anyway, because when I finally plucked up courage to tell Miss Willett a few days later (who took the news brilliantly and was amazingly supportive), she told me that Dad was no longer my legal guardian and in fact the consent would need to be obtained from the local authority as I was in their care!

# — SIXTEEN —
# THE WEDDING

We, or should I more aptly say I (a sign of things to come), planned a wedding with a special license. Alan had no money; he hadn't planned on embarking on matrimony and of course I didn't have a cent, so 'on a shoe string' was an apt description.

I wasn't any different to any other young girl; I would have loved a wedding with floating white dress and all the trimmings but this was a means to an end…I had a baby nurtured within me that needed the love and support of a family unit. That was more than enough. I would have settled for being married in a bin liner.

I went with Miss Willett to buy a wedding outfit. I'm not sure where the money came from to buy it—I have more than a sneaking suspicion it was from Miss Willett herself; she was such a kind person.

The rigours of the past few months had taken their toll in my not eating or sleeping.

I was five and a half months pregnant and bought a

straight shift-style size 8 dress and coat. It was the poshest frock I had ever had in my life and I couldn't help a tinge of sadness that it wasn't in happier circumstances that I would be wearing it. If only I could be walking down the aisle on the arm of a proud father to an adoring bridegroom waiting for me at the altar, but then we all have our dreams, don't we?

We married at Wood Green Register Office. There were eight of us altogether—Miss Willett and my father (whom Miss Willett had asked to come) to support me, Alan's mother, a close friend of his as best man and his stepbrother and sister-in-law (none of whom I had met before). I didn't know anything about his family as ours was not that sort of relationship. They were very pleasant to me.

We had the reception in a little café/restaurant near the hospital where I worked, just a simple lunch which we had pre-ordered and arranged, and we were petrified that people would order drinks rather than the obligatory one that we had paid for in advance, as we had so little money.

The owners were very kind people…I am sure the cost of what they provided was probably threefold the small budget we had placed with them but they never asked for more.

Dad didn't offer to pay for anything, ignoring what is customary for the bride's father. We certainly didn't ask… . At the reception he made a speech, wholly inappropriately really given the circumstances, but concluded 'that he wouldn't let us start married life with nothing', and with a flourish he produced an envelope out of his pocket, which he gave to Alan.

Alan's family looked impressed as of course they were meant to, and I discovered afterwards that Dad had told them that I was a young lady of independent means. (He told them that he made me an allowance, which would stop after my marriage! He lived in a Walter Mitty world.) I wish…

That £5 one-off payment certainly had stretched a long way; there had never been birthday or Christmas gifts, or cards either for that matter, for more years than I cared to remember so I certainly hadn't been a drain on his resources!

Alan's family were, naturally, in total ignorance of what had gone on in the family. I wouldn't have wanted them to know either, and, if truth be told, Alan himself knew very little too, ours had never been that close a relationship and the role of confidante had never been part of it; we really knew very little about each other.

Listening to my father playing to his audience, Miss Willett was quietly diplomatic, although I wondered what she must have been thinking. She was the only one who knew my deepest secrets, but throughout the reception she was always there, slipping an arm round me, reassuring, giving me much needed moral support.

I knew she was disappointed that this had happened and, irrationally perhaps, I felt sad that I had let her down and betrayed her faith in me, but, as always, she showed me nothing but kindness and warmth…

After Dad's speech, even knowing him as I did, I found myself wondering whether indeed he was going to help us with our start in married life, possibly as a way of making amends, albeit in a monetary way. It would have been such a great help to us with nowhere to live, no money, and a baby due so quickly.

I had left my job at the hospital only the day before I was married, so loathe was I to break away from such a happy phase in my life.

At least my induction into nursing would stand me in good stead when I eventually returned to the training but of course that wasn't in my vision then, nor for a great many years. I was sad to be leaving. It was the first time in many years I had begun to find the real me that had been buried somewhere along with all the hurt. Whilst nursing I had started to consider myself to have a value in life…

As Alan opened the envelope in a quiet moment, I was quietly optimistic, waiting for a bundle of notes or a welcome cheque to emerge.

It contained a ten-pound note.

And thus I started married life.

. Alan was a kind man but very immature, and I genuinely think he had thought no further than that we were getting married. He hadn't considered the inevitable changes to his own lifestyle (which was that of a confirmed bachelor) this would bring about. Following our wedding, we spent the night in a B & B in South Wales (Dad's ten pound note probably just covered it), and then he took me back to the digs he lived in, in Leighton Buzzard, which was a working man's café, dumped me and went to work.

The owners of this café bed and breakfast were an Irish couple, very friendly but totally ill-equipped to deal with a young pregnant girl, under their feet indoors all day. The surroundings were really only suited to their clientele (namely working men) and for that matter they too (the guys who lived here) were very ill at ease when I was around. They were more used to f—ing and blinding than watching their ps and qs! It was far from ideal.

I was starting my married life, a child bride, pregnant, with no family or friends to support me and the stark reality was that, as young as I was, whatever I wanted I was going to have to get out and find for myself, as my new husband clearly didn't have the motivation to do it for me or indeed with me.

## —SEVENTEEN—
# NEST MAKING

I went flat hunting! The realisation very quickly hit me that we didn't have very much money. Alan of course had his MG to pay for, which made a great indent in his weekly pay packet; there was absolutely no way he was parting with it! He hadn't planned on having a wife and forthcoming baby to support—as a single person just paying for digs he was fine; now this was a very different story.

The only flat I could find which was remotely within our price range, (£3 6s 0d a week to be exact) was above a wool shop. I saw a notice for it displayed in the shop window and when I called in to find out about it thought they were very amenable. (Most prospective landlords had terrified me by stating no children; no pets and a multitude of other minuses before I could even get the first word out!) I quickly found out why, in this instance, that was not the case.

The entrance to the flat was by a separate door to the left of the shop, down a passageway and then up a flight of stairs. As we started up these stairs the most awful smell of urine pervaded the air.

At the top of the stairs was a small box room in which sat a young girl in an armchair, wearing only jumper and knickers. She obviously had the most profound disabilities—clearly double-jointed, her lower limbs were suspended over her shoulder, which was a strange sight. She was without speech, omitting only screeches, and was clearly incontinent.

The only other item in this small room apart from the chair was an electric bar-type fire on full, facing the chair. The temperature was like that of a hot house and dried the urine which fell onto the chair and surrounding floor constantly, hence the most horrendous smell

The landlord told me that this was his daughter; she had had a reaction to milk as a baby, hence her current disabilities. He explained that although thirteen she had the mental age of a nine-month-old baby. Whilst they were at the shop, i.e. from 8.30 a.m. to 5.30 p.m. she remained on this chair in the room.

He said that his son too also suffered from the same condition although not so severely but I didn't at that time see him.

As a sixteen-year-old and with no experience whatsoever of profound disabilities, I am highly ashamed to admit now that Sylvia (as I believe was her name) terrified me and the smell was making me gag. I suppose that he was so accustomed to it that he didn't notice.

I wanted to run as far away as I could but instead we carried on down the passage to the flat.

Once inside the scenario wasn't much better; the last tenants who had quit some while before, I gathered, had been an Italian family with lots of children and the place was absolutely filthy. Rubbish was littered everywhere and the walls in the kitchen were just inches thick in grease.

It was a nightmare. I think the landlord had completely given up on letting the place; there were other problems too, but at the time they weren't visible to me. It would have taken a pretty desperate person to take it on. I wasn't that desperate!

I made my excuses and left, averting my eyes as I went past that room and down the stairs. Back in the street I started sobbing.

Whether it was pity for this poor young girl and the life she was leading, fear for the unborn child inside me because of my unsuccessful abortion attempts or just my sense of anti-climax I really don't know, but I couldn't wait to put as much distance between 43a Lake Street and myself as I could.

My options were running out.

There was just nowhere. I couldn't stay where I was, it wasn't fair on anyone and we didn't really have enough money for two of us in digs anyway.

The few places to rent that would take children were way out of our price range, Alan didn't really want to know, but would go along with what I sorted out (which proved to be the way of life throughout our marriage I guess) and so, with the utmost trepidation, I went back to the flat and agreed to take it.

It was furnished of sorts. Every day I would leave the digs armed with cleaning utensils (very kindly loaned by the owners), mountains of cleaning items and make my way accompanied by the strangest looks, mop buckets clattering through the town centre and up Lake Street, a distance of probably a mile or so. Then I scrubbed myself senseless, returning exhausted to the digs at night. Gradually paint pots and brushes replaced the cleaning items. I had never done anything like this in my life before but this was going to be 'my home' and I was nest-making.

I was still frightened of Sylvia—I suppose in ignorance really—but from rushing past her room, head looking the other way, I progressed to smiling. I still couldn't come to terms with the stench on the stairs and landing but as soon as I shut the front door of the flat, the smell disappeared (well almost!) and I was such a busy little bee.

Came the time when I felt it was almost fit for habitation, I took Alan to see it. Whilst visibly shocked (although I had given him the benefit of forewarning him) at Sylvia, to his credit he seemed almost enthusiastic about the flat and so, that weekend, we moved our bits and bobs, ferrying them stuck out of the roof of the MG through the town—to start our married life together in our own little home.

## —EIGHTEEN—
## SETBACKS

I was six months pregnant and felt it was time to register with a doctor. I was lucky to find one that was warm, caring, not critical with regard to the level of pregnancy I had reached without any care, or judgmental about my age as others had tended to be, or so I felt.

My life was beginning to settle down. I found too that I was eligible for maternity allowance of, I think, £4 something a week; it was a fortune to me! I hadn't earned very much at the hospital and by the time I'd paid for my board at the hostel there wasn't much left. We would just about scrape through on Alan's money but there was absolutely nothing spare to allow me to think of baby things and so on. (I think my allowance from Dad must have been a little late that week/month/year!! —I wish!)

Thus this allowance book was like manna from heaven; it was my passport to buy the things I had been looking at longingly in shop windows, like baby clothes—which

I hitherto hadn't worked out how I was going to afford—and some second-hand baby equipment.

And there was one other thing which I was absolutely desperate for, which seemed to go hand in glove with my newfound independence, only this time no one but no one would take it away from me.

It took a trip to Brick Lane in London to find him—a scraggy black bundle of fur, not much bigger than my hand, I brought my new little Waggy Mark II back to our home, my cup of joy really did runneth over!

How can things be going so well and then suddenly in the space of just a few short weeks go radically wrong?

Alan and I had really just started to get to know each other, doing what in normal circumstances you do at the onset of a relationship and were just becoming comfortable in each other's company, sharing a home. We had such a lot to learn.

Waggy II became really ill; he was having the most awful fits and the vet felt he wasn't even then old enough to have left his mother; he diagnosed distemper and explained that this was the drawback to buying animals in places like street markets…I had bought with my heart, not my head. It didn't help me; I loved and wanted him so much—he was a stepping stone into my moving forward into my new life, a security blanket. Friends and family I didn't have, but in this little bundle of fluff I could lavish care and attention and he would return it to me tenfold.

The vet tried very hard to save him, but he was just too weak and too young and died.

I was inconsolable. I felt this was an omen! Perhaps it was.

In the same week, Alan returned from working looking decidedly ill at ease. After a while he told me that he was going to work abroad for approximately five months.

Totally shocked, I naturally made the assumption he meant at a later date. It was inconceivable to me that he could mean anything else; by now I was seven and a half months pregnant, but it transpired it was an imminent departure, a fait accompli.

He mumbled excuses that it would be the only way we could manage to save any money but I realised that in reality this was something he just really wanted (and had always wanted) to do. It was a feature of his job as an industrial radiographer that he had always been enthusiastic about. He had been waiting for the opportunity, and, if the truth be told, this was more important than supporting me through the birth of what was conceivably our child.

It was a good, steady job and he enjoyed it. Instead of taking pictures of someone's appendages, he took the same of pipelines, aircraft and other objects, which as a layman, were hardly things to get excited about. Much of this sort of work featured in the oil business, the vast oil lines of the Gulf and the rigs of the North Sea.

I didn't want him to go and yet, on the other hand, how could I stand in his way? After all, in my heart of hearts I owed him so much, my sanity really—he had shown me a way forward.

Inwardly deeply hurt and yes, I must admit, I was very frightened too of being on my own in my present condition without a friendly face or any family to turn to. The realisation too that he placed me obviously well below this new venture in his priorities only endorsed what I knew in my heart of hearts anyway—that he wasn't ready to assume the role of husband and father and the responsibilities that came with it. But who could blame him? Certainly not me and so I said nothing and went along with his preparations and mounting excitement.

His firm took me to the airport to wave him off and, as the plane disappeared into the skyline, I realised that, married or not, I really was 'on my own'!

# —NINETEEN—
# LONELINESS

On the day he flew out I was just eight months pregnant, and I felt totally rejected and alone.

It happens to lots of people, I know, that their partner isn't around, but they usually have the support of family and friends to fall back on and were a bit worldlier and in all probability older than me. I was in a strange town knowing no one.

It was a lonely time. I painted up old furniture for my nursery, trying to while away the hours.

I had gone belatedly to antenatal classes and met one or two people there who were friendly but not to the extent of spending time in each other's company.

The time just dragged. I used to go out walking for miles and altogether had a great deal too much time in which to reflect and brood.

I became paranoid and full of remorse that, because I hadn't wanted my baby and even worse, tried to get rid of it, God would punish me by giving it the most dreadful deformities or even worse, taking it away from me. I was convinced that this was going to happen, spending the interminable days and even worse, the nights crying, distraught at the prospect.

I discovered that Alan was no communicator either; there were no letters of support during the whole six-month period he was away, just a couple of postcards. I had no contact whatsoever with Dad or, so it seemed, anyone. Even Miss Willett seemed to have deserted me.

Alan's firm bought me a present. I think it could be said that they felt a pang of remorse or possibly guilt at sending him away although I have no doubt whatsoever that Alan was a more than willing party. When someone from the office brought round his weekly wage packet, he had obviously testified at first-hand to his bosses the picture I represented—a lonely young girl, with tears always just below the surface.

It was a poodle, unfortunately the most highly-strung, interbred specimen I had ever seen, costing an absolute fortune I gather. (I expect it was a small price to pay for their obviously pricked consciences.) The poor creature was a complete nervous wreck; it scratched all day and every day, wouldn't walk on a lead, wouldn't eat any form of dog food, and was a complete nightmare.

It had a pedigree and a name that was so long it was unpronounceable so I called it Ja Ja.

It cowed in the corner, crying—talk about like attracting like! I spent most of the time crying too. We must have made a right pair but at least it distracted me from my own self-pity and I immersed myself in eczema treatments and special diets. The breeder must definitely have seen them coming and counted his blessings to have offloaded it.

It was at this time I discovered one of the other problems with the flat too.

Barry, the landlord's son.

He spent most of his time working in the wool shop with or without his father present. He used to stare at me when I was going in and out, usually smiled but said very little.

I always felt somehow he was keeping track of my movements. His father had told me that he suffered from the same problem as Sylvia but to a much lesser degree.

I had for some time felt that someone was gaining access to the flat as things often seemed to have been moved, like articles of clothing and personal belongings. Foodstuff too seemed to disappear.

I thought I was being paranoid until one day I had gone out, forgotten something and returned to find Barry mooching around inside. I don't know who was the most startled, him or me, but he ran out and I had the locks changed.

Having someone in my space when I wasn't there was unpleasant but nothing to his other traits. At the rear of the shop was a yard, which was accessible both to them and to me. I had a washing line there and I believe there was an outside toilet for the shop use. My windows overlooked it. I became aware that Barry was spending long hours standing in the yard just staring up at my windows, which was very disconcerting.

Even worse, he started defecating on the floor in the yard, which was horrendous. I couldn't hang out my washing without walking over huge piles of stinking turds and I realised that there was no way I would be able to put my baby outside to sleep there.

I was in a complete quandary. I was now in my final stages of pregnancy, I certainly had nowhere else to go and I doubt the energy to do so on my own even if an opportunity presented itself.

In the total absence of a man around or anyone who could sort it out for me, I plucked up courage and told his father (although he really couldn't have missed it going outside to the loo himself, and they stored their rubbish there too), who said he would 'deal with it'.

It was obviously not the first time the situation had arisen and quite possibly why other tenants had left, and there was the most almighty row in the shop and I suspect, although I hope that I am wrong, that, judging by the screams obviously coming from Barry, he had given his son a good hiding.

It changed nothing: he obviously saw me now as an enemy and scowled and muttered obscenities under his breath every time he saw me. He continued to behave as an animal, and to stare malevolently up at my windows for hours at a time, I think his parents periodically cleared up the terrible mess, but I could obviously no longer use the yard and for that matter didn't feel safe in my house, even after having the locks changed and having safety chains fitted as an extra precaution. I was really frightened.

I had heard nothing from Dad in all this time. I of course didn't know Alan's family, and having met them for the first time at my wedding, had made no further contact with them so there were no male influences I could turn to for support in my life. Apart from a couple of girls I had met who I had become friendly with, both of whom were pregnant, I didn't have anyone to fall back on.

I didn't have a telephone, so was really rather isolated. Not surprisingly, I became increasingly worried that I wouldn't know when I was in labour, and I fretted as to how I would get to the hospital or call an ambulance: calling down to Barry in the shop wasn't really an option!

# −TWENTY−
# FEAR

My delivery date came but nothing happened; one week went by and another was fast disappearing. I went to the hospital for a check-up (this involved quite a trek incidentally from Leighton Buzzard to Aylesbury on the bus).

Acquainting them with the fact that I was living on my own was probably instrumental in their deciding to take me in and induce me—so that was one less worry at least, although I was terrified of the actual birth and continued to live with the fear that something might be wrong with the baby. This was a secret that I and I alone had had to live with through those past months.

I trundled back on the bus, took my neurotic puppy to kennels as arranged by Alan's firm (at their expense).

To be fair, Ja Ja had improved vastly but still scratched all day long. The vet had shaved him so he looked like something out of a horror movie, poor thing, and I knew that—in leaving him—all my work over the past few weeks would have been for nothing. But there was nothing else I could do short of sneaking him into the hospital and, believe me, as the only living thing whom I had in the world right then who seemed to love me, I would have done so if there was any possible way!

With heavy heart and filled with utter desolation and loneliness, I packed my bag and set off again for the hospital.

The sheer isolation and terror I was feeling engulfed me and I cried quietly to myself for the duration of the long bus ride, wishing that an enormous hole in the road would appear and swallow us up!

At the hospital I was put in a side ward. Everyone was so busy rushing about! If they wondered why this young girl had no one with her to hold her hand and give her moral support, they didn't ask; they obviously drew their own conclusions. Ironically, they were the wrong ones but they might as well have been! I had a husband in name only. I had two weeks to go to my seventeenth birthday but probably looked younger.

The consultant came to see me to explain the procedure of rupturing the membranes. He was kind, fatherly almost; perhaps he judged how frightened I was. He warned me, however, that, due to my slightness I would probably have a long labour. 'Not necessarily a bad one,' he was quick to add.

I wanted to scream, 'If it delays the inevitable moment when I see my baby and the harm I have inflicted on it,' as I was so certain was the case, 'it can go on forever!' But of course that was my inner turmoil and outwardly I just nodded shyly.

The hours dragged on interminably. I wished they had

put me in a ward; at least I would have had things to watch and probably someone to talk to instead of enduring this quiet seclusion, which gave me just what I didn't need—time to dwell on my fears, causing them to escalate all the time.

They broke my waters late afternoon and left me once again to my own devices.

The only diversion was an orderly who brought in tea. She reminded me in some ways of Susie's mum; perhaps it was the accent, she was probably German too I think. Plonking the tray down, she turned to look me up and down before saying, 'Having a baby are you…? Good God, you're only a baby yourself, what on earth is the world coming to?' She tutted to herself and left the room.

Fortunately, those thoughtless words of unkindness were the only ones spoken to me during my stay at the hospital and everyone else was kindness itself.

The midwives drifted in and out of the room checking on my progress (or rather lack of it) but at around ten p.m. they told me I was having contractions…I wouldn't have known so it was probably a good job I was in a safe place. Had I been at home, it wouldn't have occurred to me to go to the hospital.

Of course as the evening turned into nightfall they got worse and I must have presented a sad little figure. One of the midwives befriended me, and stayed with me all of the time (I presume it must have been a quiet night, not too many babies making their entrance! Or maybe she was just sensitive to my extreme need, talking and reassuring, calming me.) She was about the age my mum would have been.

In those twilight hours I poured out my heart to her, my tormented soul knowing no bounds as I told her how I had allowed harm to befall my baby. With the pain secondary to the terror I was feeling, in between contractions, she held me in her arms, quietly soothing, exuding compassion and support.

## TWENTY-ONE
## New Beginnings

And as the dawn came in, the silence of the night broken by the chorus of awakening birds who seemed to be offering a greeting, my daughter came into this world, wailing indignantly at the undignified entrance, the most exquisitely perfect, beautiful being that I had ever seen in my life.

I don't know who cried the most: myself, the midwife or my indignant daughter, but they were tears of untold joy, of new beginnings and as I cradled her in my arms I knew with absolute certainty that, as long as I had breath in my body, she would always be enveloped with love, security and warmth. Together we turned another chapter of our life.

In keeping with the time of day she had made her entrance, I called her Dawn (I hadn't dared let myself think of names before).

I moved in to a ward with other new mums, a laughing, joyous place—new babies seem to bring out the best in everyone.

When the consultant did his morning round, and saw me sitting there, he made the assumption that rupturing the membranes hadn't induced my labour, so convinced had he been that I was in for a long haul!

And, beaming from ear to ear, I showed him my new daughter with his congratulations ringing in my ears.

I had told my fellow inmates that my husband was abroad; whether they believed it or not I'm not sure but they were great, and we all, with first babies, went through a learning curve together.

I think that my new daughter could have carried out the teaching process herself though, I am sure she had been this way before, so streetwise was she!

My beautiful little girl had the most amazing mop of wavy, dark hair curling down into the nape of her neck. So prolific was it that more than one person enquired if my husband was English!! Fortunately I had a mop of dark hair as well so the assumption was that she took after her mum, a good job because Alan was very fair.

I wanted to share my joy with everyone. I rang Susie and Miss Willett, wrote to everyone else I could think of.

From Alan's firm came a beautiful spray of red roses, ostensibly from him, although I think more likely they had put his name to them.

Visiting times were lonely (doting new dads and beaming grandparents surging in to share the joys with their loved ones) because I didn't really have anyone, but I immersed myself in my beautiful daughter, marvelling at her perfection and it just didn't matter. I was quite unable to believe my good fortune.

Susie did come to see me, her arms full of beautiful clothes and a wonderful teddy and even goodwill messages from her mum. Miss Willett too suddenly appeared one day, her smiling face peeping round the door and I realised how much I had missed her.

There were lots of cards from Alan's family, from my aunts, even from the friends I had made and a matinee jacket my Auntie Nell had knitted.

Everyone was so kind, even my midwife friend called in most days for a few minutes' natter and I was very lucky.

Out of gratitude for the absolute support she had given me, well over and above her expected role, I got one of the husbands of my ward companion to buy some perfume for me.

Tucking it into the corner of my daughter's cot in anticipation of her daily visit, I attached the following little note to it:

> This little gift I'm sending you,
> With thanks from me and my mum too,
> For helping her, and helping me,
> To make my entrance gracefully.
> So because you helped me to be born,
> I'm sending this, with love from Dawn.

Hardly the Poet Laureate! I wonder if she had even the smallest idea of how much she did for me, just by being there, listening, supporting. She loved the poem and said she was going to frame it. Maybe it's tucked away forgotten in a drawer somewhere and if she ever reads this, she'll dig it out and think of my little daughter and me.

I didn't hear from Dad.

# —TWENTY-TWO—
# CHILD'S PLAY

Ten days later my daughter and I were on the way home. It sometimes takes something in life to give you a jolt into reality, a purpose to live for. For me this was it and I settled down to life with my newborn offspring as if we had been together for years.

Of course every mum thinks her baby is the best in the world! But Dawn unquestionably was: she was the most easy-going, placid baby, which made my induction into motherhood so easy. She never cried, she slept like a dream, and lay contentedly in her pram.

This little paragon of virtue had undoubtedly been round the block before. What with my baby and my puppy (who had survived the rigours of the kennels amazingly well), my cup ranneth over.

I had my seventeenth birthday a week later. No one remembered it and I had only my wonderful new daughter to share it with, but somehow it didn't matter a jot. With my daughter snug in her pram, my now rejuvenated puppy jogging along beside us, we walked for miles. Surely I was the happiest and luckiest girl in the world and that terrible birthday just four years before, at the peak of my unhappiness, seemed a lifetime away.

One hears and reads about such awful things that new mothers can face, but fortunately not me. The most traumatic thing that happened to me in those early first weeks was that I forgot Dawn and left her in her pram outside Woolworths in the town! Going home, I had immersed myself in chores until the sickening reality hit me, several hours later, that I had forgotten her, and I tore back into the town to find her still sleeping soundly exactly where I'd left her, none the worse for her extended outing.

Life went smoothly, and my little family certainly had a glut of fresh air; pushing the pram with Ja Ja on his lead, we'd walk for miles and miles. We didn't have any money but we had something far more precious.

I had sent Dad a note to tell him about Dawn (it's always there, under the surface, that need to be loved). A few weeks later he came to see his granddaughter and me, only I don't think he'd really thought of her that way.

I scrubbed and polished my little flat until it gleamed but I don't think he even noticed, even admonishing me for living in a hovel! He should have seen my broom cupboard of a room at the hostel! And, apart from a cursory glance in the pram, he didn't seem to notice Dawn either.

We made uncomfortable small talk for a couple of hours; the only thing of any consequence to come out of it was that WW had gone back to live in Lancashire, voluntarily or forced he didn't enlarge upon and I didn't ask. They were, it seemed from his conversation, quite settled in Kent.

As we struggled to make polite conversation, it was as if we were strangers. No one would have believed we were father and daughter and that this was the first time he had seen his only grandchild. It was purely a duty visit and, surreptitiously, he kept looking at his watch.

Talking of watches, he went down the road to buy me one because I didn't have anything from which to tell the time in the flat, and then hurriedly made his excuses and left.

I wasn't sorry to see him go, although I felt sad that he couldn't have at least made the pretence of being pleased to make the acquaintance of his little granddaughter; he hadn't even held her.

Dawn thrived, and surpassed every baby book with her development—I'm sure she was a thirty-year-old midget posing as a three-month-old baby so streetwise did she seem to be. I blossomed in the praise of my parenting abilities and once again my self-esteem and confidence started spiralling upwards again.

I had sent Alan lots of photos of her and I was looking forward so much to his return—particularly as he didn't write, which would have helped bridge the distance between us.

# —TWENTY-THREE—
# REUNIONS

She was five months old when he returned, looking tanned and a lot healthier than when he had left. (Alan was very prone to skin disorders and the sunny climate had obviously suited him.) He was very happy to see us and meet his new daughter at last; he fell in love with her straightaway. How could he not? I was so excited that we would now be a real little family.

Making love on that first evening I thought my happiness was finally complete, we were together again as a family. I was prepared to give him my heart.

I was due to start a period imminently (literally within a couple of days) so we didn't practise birth control. Only that period didn't arrive and the reality dawned that I was pregnant again. So much for a second honeymoon period for getting to know each other, not that we ever had a first one!

We took Dawn to meet her grandmother—a bit of a squash in the two-seater MG with a baby and a dog but we managed.

She lived in a tiny little one-up and one-down cottage in the beautiful Forest of Dean. I don't know how I can really describe my mother-in-law…a bit of a recluse, certainly eccentric, she had had a very hard life and it was difficult to crack the artificial veneer that surrounded her, but I tried very hard.

It was so important to me that she should like me and I really worked to accomplish this. She was a prime candidate for *The Good Life*; very self-sufficient, she kept chickens, grew her own vegetables and fruit and could, and indeed did, turn her hand to everything.

Dawn wasn't a first grandchild; Alan's twin brother (whom I hadn't met as he lived abroad with his family) had several children, and his stepbrother (who had come to our wedding) had a grown-up family too.

Had she been the first, however, I don't think it would have made a great deal of difference. Alan's mother wasn't one to show any emotion, although her heart was in the right place. I think the right way to describe my mother-in-law was a lady of very strong character!

My first induction into life in the Forest of Dean was glancing out of the window into the garden where I had placed my daughter to enjoy the country air, to see the biggest pig I had ever set eyes on with his head in the carrycot, obviously deciding whether Dawn was lunch! (Good job the book and film *Hannibal* wasn't around then; as an avid reader my life would never have been the same again!)

Alan and his mum were nowhere to be seen, so there was nothing else for it.

I did what all self-respecting mothers would do; armed with the broom and the carving knife (although goodness only knows what I was going to do with it!) I charged at the offending creature like an African warrior, quite expecting to see him lift his head with a dismembered limb in his mouth, instead of which, as the broom hit him with a resounding whack, and the knife was poised ready for the kill, the poor thing let out a great squeal and careered off down the garden with me in hot pursuit.

I learnt later that he was the 'pet' of the next-door neighbour and as gentle as a lamb. Bet he didn't ever cross the boundary into the adjoining garden again and he must have thought he was nearer to pork chops than he had ever been in his life before!!

But worse was yet to come.

Once again, my husband and mother-in-law had wandered off somewhere, when I heard a tremendous banging against the wall of the cottage. Summoning up my courage, I ventured outside and it was emanating from an old tin bath that was hanging upside down against the wall, literally crashing up and down.

This time, armed with the rolling pin which just happened to be handy, I lifted up the bath…underneath was a newly slaughtered chicken with its head hanging off. Obviously the poor thing's nerves were having their final fling.

As an out-and-out townie, it was incomprehensible to me that my mother-in-law took the meaning 'oven ready' as being from the farmyard literally into the pot. Culling tomorrow's Sunday roast was as natural to her and indeed to most country-bred people as was my hitherto concept of the same Sunday roast, namely in a supermarket freezer cabinet!

The poor thing was flapping its wings in a last desperate rebellion against its fate.

Needless to say, lunch was off for my part, a trend I maintained when we made future visits too. Food sources were all too often (to my over active imagination) suspect!

What were off too were visits to the loo for me.

The toilet was a tin with some Jeyes Fluid in it, in a dark, rank shed in the garden. By comparison, an Elson would have been positively sophisticated. I don't think it was emptied particularly regularly and, try as I might, I couldn't bring myself to use it. I just about managed the large potty in the bedroom (being pregnant didn't really help, since I wanted to wee every two minutes!) during the night but no way was I venturing near this evil-smelling concoction—I would have expected something to crawl out and grab me. The woods at the bottom of the garden were far more preferable! At least I 'knew' it was a stinging nettle attacking my rear anatomy!

My life seemed to have been blighted by loos. Avoiding them to keep away from unwelcome amorous advances, then because of the fear of the bodies in the adjoining room at my aunt's undertakers and now this...wonder what an analyst would make of it.

I didn't confess to my mother-in-law that I was pregnant again; I had a more than healthy respect for her sharp tongue, but I was to realise as I got to know her better, that her bark was far worse than her bite.

We renewed our contact with Alan's stepbrother and family too; they lived in the south and were friendly and welcoming. With two children in their late teens similar in age to me, they seemed a really caring happy family and I enjoyed their company very much.

Ironically, the reason for Alan's leaving me to work abroad whilst I was having Dawn, namely to earn some money for us, hadn't materialised and he had returned without a penny and indeed owing the company money. The temptations of the Arab Emirates had taken their toll and new cameras, gold, and even a Persian rug had joined us. The money would have been a lot more use, but, never mind, we all make mistakes.

We didn't have much money but we were managing and getting to know each other in the ways most people do before they set up home together. I felt we were doing all right and it was a happy time for all of us.

# TWENTY-FOUR
# COMFORTABLE SHOES

This pregnancy was completed by the book, early antenatal care, and care and attention to myself being in very sharp contrast to my first when I never had so much as an iron tablet!

Alan was working all over the place; I knew he was very keen to return abroad but I did offer token resistance, feeling that he should get to know his daughter, and, for that matter, me a little better.

In my blossoming confidence, I offered up suggestions that he should also wave goodbye to the car as it was totally impractical, but he wasn't ready for that one!

I suppose I would describe my relationship with Alan rather as a comfortable shoe. He was totally devoid of passion about anything, had a mammoth chip on his shoulder about life generally, but wasn't prepared to do anything about it. However, his good points were that he was exceedingly kind and loyal and, whilst not loving him in the deepest sense of the word, with my heart missing a beat when he came in the room, I was one hundred per cent committed to giving everything I'd got to the relationship and, for want of a better description, being 'a good wife'.

My life with Dawn was a delight; she was as bright as a button, learning something new every day, probably because I spent every waking moment with her—talking to her, treating her more as though she was a person rather than a baby. You'd almost have expected her to get up and do the hoovering!

Alan was working away from home but in the UK, which I think was a reluctant compromise on his part. I was five months into a very healthy pregnancy. Even Barry, my malevolent neighbour downstairs, wasn't troubling me as he had used to before Alan's return.

# —TWENTY-FIVE—
# Crisis

The day started as any other—whipping around the housework, taking Dawn and Ja Ja for their long walk. When I returned to the flat several hours later, I felt intuitively that everything wasn't well, but there were no signs of anything amiss.

I took Dawn and we went for a nap.

I awoke to overwhelming wetness.

Glancing down, I was lying in a pool of blood, alone, with no telephone.

I grabbed my sleeping daughter and tried to go downstairs to get to a phone to call for help. I was losing so much blood that I had to return to grab a couple of towelling nappies to try and stem the flow. Goodness knows what I must have looked like, wandering down the street but it was the last thing on my mind!

I called my doctor, who arrived speedily and in turn, called an ambulance. He was also kind enough to call a friend with whom I could leave my precious daughter.

I knew that he felt I was losing the baby but he didn't say so.

This time I was taken to Dunstable, even further than Aylesbury. I was in complete shock, but more from fear of having to leave the most precious thing in my life than with the preoccupation of what was happening. It was incomprehensible to me to have to be away from my 'Dawnie'.

Alan was located and rushed back, naturally very concerned but more with the realities of the situation, I felt, than with what was happening to me. I think his difficulty was that he just didn't feel adept at looking after Dawn and, to be fair, he had had very little to do with her care, other than being reassuring to me. The friend who had come to my rescue had a small baby herself as well as health problems and just wasn't well enough to keep Dawn other than for a few hours.

Still bleeding heavily and obviously in shock, by now I was on a drip. I wanted Alan to be assertive, tell me he would manage, but I have to say he completely failed me. Panic-stricken at the thought of looking after a five-month-old baby, he 'arranged' for the wife of someone he worked with to take her, someone I had never even met…and was totally oblivious to the anguish I was feeling at being separated from my lifeline. He almost cheerfully said, 'She has four boys, has always wanted a daughter so Dawn will be in good hands!'

This stranger could have been an Alice Mark 2 or even worse, as far as I was concerned. Given a choice, I would have left the hospital at that moment but was so weak that I could hardly move…and this was to be where I would remain for the following month!

The doctors diagnosed something called a Placenta Praevia which they told me could be extremely dangerous both for the baby and for the mother too.

Initially they kept me hanging in there on a day-by-day basis, not directly answering my pleas to go home and thus I thought every day would be the one I did escape. Being without my baby was like someone cutting out my heart—I missed her so much.

I do have to say I soon learned that the lady who was looking after her, Chris she was called, was a lovely lady and idolised Dawn (how could she not!).

She brought her to see me so that I could see she was happy and cared for, but it mattered not a jot; every second she was away from me was too long and she was changing almost daily and I was missing it all!

In reality, the hospital planned to keep me there until my pregnancy went to term, over four months, but I was distraught and my mental health was deteriorating. I couldn't eat, I was so depressed.

In normal circumstances, perhaps with a loving and caring family to support me, it would have been endurable but mine wasn't a normal circumstance. I became paranoid that I was losing my daughter, and although I very much wanted the new life nurtured inside me, so nearly lost, everything was eclipsed by my desperation to get back to Dawn. I was prepared to do anything, even if it meant the radical step of discharging myself, which at that time seemed my only way out of that bed.

In the end, there was no need to be quite so rash. The consultant and nursing staff, so kind and sympathetic to my plight, allowed me to go home with the strict proviso that I rest most of the time, to return post-haste if there was the slightest bleeding or problem and to remain in constant contact with my GP.

It was a small price to pay to get back to 'my girl'.

In those four weeks I had left a baby and returned to a little girl. At ten months Dawn was amazing, chatting away, and had even come out of nappies. (She had been spoilt rotten, I knew, and with four boys in the house pampering to her every whim every time she fluttered her eyelashes she'd had a wonderful time.)

Thank you, Chris, for your lifeline, even if it wasn't wanted in the first place!

I lasted a month; I was sensible, did as I was told, rested, saw my doctor several times a week and was almost lulled into a false sense of security. I made forward plans. I arranged for Dawn to be cared for by my friend (as she had offered) this time when I actually went in to have the baby, to be supported by Alan of course. I hoped for a quick delivery before returning to my own nest.

I woke up in the night and was bleeding again; Alan, to his credit, had remained at home, working locally so I had him for my immediate support—no dashing out this time. He called for an ambulance, but by the time it arrived I was having strong labour pains.

I was almost relieved; at least the baby would have a chance of survival, early as it was, whereas just stopping the bleeding as had happened before meant that no one knew really what harm was befalling my unborn child. The consultant had warned me before that a Placenta Praevia in most cases required a Caesarean section.

Very quickly, my little baby came into this world. A tiny

scrap of humanity, nearly three months premature, another little girl but weighing well less than three pounds, she was christened straight away. I called her Debbie.

Looking down at this tiny scrap fighting so desperately for her life, tears streamed down my face. We all face a lifetime of hurdles ahead of us, but somehow it seemed so unfair that she had to face the biggest hurdle of all within the first very precious minutes of life—that of survival.

No one was optimistic; she was so fragile, yet she clung on by a thread, a real fighter. Slowly but surely, the minutes ticked into hours and the hours into days and she hung on in there and people changed their pessimism for very real hope.

I went home, leaving my tiny little bundle in an incubator, but, I knew, in the excellent care of the medical team there.

## — TWENTY-SIX —
## DESERTION AGAIN

It was not the most appropriate time for Alan to be off abroad again, this time not quite so far—working in Rotterdam—so in theory he would be able to get home more often. In my heart of hearts, as hurt as I inwardly felt, I took the course of least resistance. If he didn't have the sensitivity to know how much we needed him, I certainly wasn't going to spell it out to him.

I know that he had a job to do but I am sure, given the circumstances, there was a degree of flexibility as to where he did it. I don't question for a moment that he loved his family but it was as if what *he* wanted to do must always come first and he seemed almost detached from the realities of a wife and two small babies. I really needed him at home to help and support me through this difficult time while Debbie was in hospital, her future still not guaranteed. The sheer practicalities of getting in and out to her, because of living such a distance from the hospital, made life difficult but my pride wouldn't let me beg him.

To give Debbie the best possible start (she was being fed at that time through a tiny tube), it meant my expressing breast milk with a pump and taking it to the hospital.

This was peak summer, we didn't have a fridge at home to store it in, or the money to buy one, and so every day would see Dawn and I embarking on an hour's bus ride to Luton, followed by a walk of a couple of miles at the other end to the hospital to deliver the milk, then an about-turn, reversing the process. It was totally exhausting, taking all day, every day.

The big and the little milkmaid!

Dawn was eleven months and one day old when her sister was born; she was already walking and insisted on doing just that, so it used to take us hours, her tiny legs never giving in.

Debbie thrived, although she was still in an incubator. I used to marvel at this perfect little creature with the tiniest of limbs.

I hadn't as yet held her although I used to sit holding her hand whilst Dawn created havoc in the ward. Fortunately the nurses adored her and use to vie with each other to play with her; it was a great help and they were all very relaxed given the monumental amount of responsibility and dedication they shouldered in running this premature baby unit.

The long-awaited day came, when on our daily milk round the nurses placed Debbie gently in my arms. I hadn't even held her when she was born so it was a strange sensation. I loved her desperately of course, but until that moment she hadn't felt as if she was mine.

Now I could really begin to look forward to us being together as a family.

The flat wasn't suitable for two babies, it was just too small. I had accepted not having anywhere to dry clothes or to leave a baby outside in a pram because of the Barry problem which hadn't really abated. I had just learnt to live with it, with the extra security to my locks and so on. I used the launderette dryers but they cost a lot of money, and, on a tight budget, with two little babies instead of one this would be a major problem. I wanted Debbie to have the best possible start, somewhere she could sleep outside in her pram. Quite simply I wanted a garden, and so I started the rounds of the letting agents again.

By now, incidentally, Debbie was being fed on Carnation Milk at the hospital, and gaining weight at a far greater rate than when she had been on breast milk. (Perhaps all the travelling backwards and forwards had taken much of the goodness out of it. I don't know—it had certainly taken most of the energy out of me.) The pressure of the milk round was taken away from me, so there was a little time for flat hunting.

# TWENTY-SEVEN
# Upping Sticks

Fate must have been on my side because I found the perfect spot, a little farm gate house situated in a tiny canal-side village about ten miles from Leighton Buzzard.

Surrounded by fields and rural beauty, I felt that this was the ideal spot for my two little girls to grow and thrive in.

It was also extremely isolated so I realised too that driving lessons would have to be a priority.

I had mixed feelings about leaving the flat. On the one hand, I wouldn't be sad to leave the bustle of the town while the ferrying of babies and shopping up flights of stairs all the time was jolly hard work. At least the next tenants (if there were any) would find a home and not a hovel. I would be leaving a good friend, but she was mobile and promised to visit, while my other friend Pauline had moved away anyway. But on the other hand it had been my first real home where I had felt secure, my very own little nest.

Another reason, which was why I had more than a twinge of sadness, was that I had got used to my funny little neighbour in that awful room downstairs and I tried to spend a few minutes with Sylvia each day, taking Dawn and Ja Ja in to see her. She definitely recognised us and her face would light up in smiles. If there were no takers for the flat, she would be alone all day again, seeing no one. I would miss her. I knew she would miss us.

There was another factor of real concern; I would have to leave my doctor's practice, and he had been a tower of strength to me. He had always treated me as a sensible, mature, young lady and a mum and I had never felt self-conscious and inhibited by my extreme youth which, if truth be told, I did with health visitors and others whom, whilst not making a direct referral to it, did so by insinuation. We'd had a good rapport and mutual respect.

I knew, with Debbie coming out of hospital very shortly, that she couldn't be in better hands. I conveyed my concerns to him and he was kind enough to say he would keep me on his panel, even making home visits; although technically it was out of his catchment area. So the last hurdle was overcome and we were 'on the move'.

I hired a van and driver and all our worldly goods were—not forgetting dog and baby—on route for our new home. Alan was too busy with his contract abroad to make the journey back, hadn't seen the house at all but was happy enough to leave all decisions to me—in short, anything for an easy life was how I construed it. I was learning independence skills fast.

And so we moved.

On the day after we moved into our new home, turning

the pages of another chapter of my life, I celebrated my eighteenth birthday, my daughter and I devouring a very huge chocolate cake in honour of the occasion.

For the second time in less than two years, here I was painting and creating a home for 'my' family. What did it matter that no one else remembered...?

It had taken three months for Debbie to join the family at home, but now here she was at just five pounds, a real little cutie pie because she was smiling away from this tiny little body, when I collected her from the hospital.

Home was a lovely place in which to bring up a family; we spent hours walking by the canal and my girls had all the fresh air they could possibly want.

Ja Ja too had suddenly discovered heaven, joining forces with the Labradors at the farm; he raced around, never on a lead, creating havoc. They were quick to pass on their bad habits too.

There was a typical village shop just across the road, owned by a very, shall we say, eccentric man called Charlie. The shop was a muddle of foods and knick-knacks, all mixed up together. Fridges seemed to be a dirty word and sausages and other fresh meats were draped around in strings on various hooks. It certainly had 'atmosphere' and would without a doubt have been an Environmental Health Officer's nightmare, but it served the needs of the community and by and large we were a pretty hardy lot for we hadn't heard of Ecoli, Listeria and Botulism and everything else in those days!

Charlie himself could well have had a part-time job as a chimney sweep judging by his appearance...enough said, but he was always cheerful, cigarette suspended from his mouth, ash dropping everywhere; he just didn't give a damn. His demeanour only ever changed and the swear words erupted when the dogs from the farm appeared, now with Ja Ja in tow (he had made a very good apprentice, agile and quick to learn).

They nipped in and whipped the string of sausages, tearing off down the road with them, with Charlie in hot pursuit, using language that would make a navvy blush, to the merriment of everyone watching.

He nearly always caught them, giving them a kick up the backsides and retrieving the sausages, but things were never quite the same for me when, following him back to the shop one day, I saw him get a dirty old cloth, wipe them off and put them back on the hook!

Definitely no more bangers and mash on my menu!

## −TWENTY-EIGHT−
# THE TEST

Debbie was very prone to chest infections necessitating regular visits to both doctor and hospital too.

Alan wasn't around to help and, with one bus coming through the village a day, things were very difficult so I took the bull by the horns and had driving lessons.

Being young, I learnt pretty quickly and if anything I was over-confident. My instructor was an elderly gentleman, not particularly strong in his tutoring skills, and I have more than a sneaking suspicion that he was a sucker for a pair of long legs (of the feminine gender of course). He didn't really exercise any discipline over my driving skills or perhaps I should say, lack of them!

However, what he lacked in his professionalism perhaps, he made up for in kindness. Whilst I had a next-door neighbour who was kind enough on occasions to stay with the girls, most of the time they were ensconced on the back seat!

In my hour's lesson prior to my test, there was a snarl-up in the high street in Aylesbury where I was due to take it, traffic congestion on both sides of the road and road works as well. It was a stalemate situation. No one was moving.

Patience never being my strong point, and fed up with waiting, I took the initiative. Nipping through with only inches to spare on either side, my wing mirror clipped a tin of paint or something similar in the hand of a workman and it catapulted over the bonnet of the car! I didn't dare slow down to see where it landed!

My instructor was not amused and muttered veiled threats under his breath at his misgivings at lending me his car for the test! Muttering something about having brown hair until he met me...

Ironically, come the time of the test, as the examiner and myself moved out of the test centre, my nerves got the better of me and, when he asked me, I said I couldn't read the number plate outside the test centre. In fact all I could read was NNN...I thought I was seeing double or treble as the case may be!!

My instructor was shaking his fist at me from across the road, muttering expletives, but doing things by the rules, the examiner had to go to another street and measure the distance with a tape measure. I sheepishly said, 'If you're going to ask me what that number is, it's—' to which he curtly responded, 'How come you can read that one at forty yards, but not the other at twenty-five?'

I don't think I drove badly at all but he failed me anyway, probably out of spite for what he considered my time-wasting, and I was really dejected because the waiting list for re-tests was over four months and I didn't have the money for more lessons anyway, so I told everyone I'd passed my test. Not that I had a vehicle to drive at that moment but I was working on it!

When I got back to the test centre, incidentally, the first car whose number plate I couldn't read was still parked and so I peered closely...surprise, surprise, the registration was NNN!

## —TWENTY-NINE—
# TEMPTATIONS

I loved my life although it was isolated and lonely. I had only made a couple of friends since my move to Bedfordshire. Whilst they didn't know of my background and those dark shadows in my life, they were kind and accepted me for what I was—which it has to be said was a whole lot more confident and happy than that lonely young girl of what seemed just a few short months ago. One has remained a very special friend throughout my life—Pauline. She too had had a baby just after the birth of Dawn, a little boy called Steven. She was rather like the sister I had always wanted. (I had one, of course, but had never been permitted by Alice to allow the love that I felt for her to show—she wasn't to be contaminated by my bad blood.) Pauline regularly came over to stay and together the two of us would use the limited buses that were available to wander all over the place…have babies, will travel, distance no object.

Neither of us had much money but we did see life, as

the saying goes. We even got as far as Great Yarmouth once, staying in a bed and breakfast.

The children played happily in the sand, paddling whilst we relaxed and sunbathed —it was idyllic! (I didn't even look longingly for a fun fair so it must have been good!)

Unfortunately, it was rather a question of, now you see her, now you don't, because one minute my friend was sitting at my side, the next she was upside down on the sand. I thought she was messing around but quickly realised she was unconscious.

The rest of our day was spent in Casualty, as it was then called, where they diagnosed heat stroke and it was serious enough for them to keep her in for a day.

I didn't realise that Great Yarmouth was ever warm enough to trigger this complaint; on the couple of occasions I have visited it in later years and spent my time shivering on the seafront ensconced in layers of clothes, it seemed utterly incomprehensible—but there you go, the wonderful climate of the great British seaside!

Where did those heat waves go? Global warming has a lot to answer for.

None the worse for our ordeal, we travelled happily home on the Green Line.

Spending so much time on my own, I lost myself in books; you always have a friend in those pages. Most young girls of my age were enjoying life to the full but I was content with mine even if my husband was an absentee one. Living in the countryside reaped its own rewards. I was anxious to learn country ways too as an out-and-out townie. I made some terrible mistakes, but by far the worst (and I still hang my head in shame at the thought) was to buy a tortoise. The pet shop told me to drill a hole through his shell to tie him up to keep him in our garden, so I did, but through the middle of his back! Not surprisingly the poor thing died. I was mortified.

Happy with my lot, there was only one thorn in my side—the car.

We had reached a stage whereby even Alan couldn't fail to appreciate that four of us and the paraphernalia two babies take, not to mention the dog (and where we went, he went) couldn't fit in the MG. He was away abroad much of the time anyway, so it sat on the drive doing nothing. He went out and bought a very posh Mini Cooper S, bright gleaming red. This was rather mean of him, bearing in mind the small point that he *thought*, because I had told him, that I had passed my driving test. Well least said…but a young inexperienced driver like me would never get insurance to drive it so he was still rendering me transportless. Leaving to go away again, he arranged for them to deliver the car, which sat magnificently on our drive saying, 'Drive me…'

It was rather like giving a child a bag of dolly mixtures he couldn't open…I tried to pretend it wasn't there but by the second day, could contain myself no longer and, leaving my sleeping daughters in the safe-keeping of my neighbour, decided to have a little run out to see Chris (the lady who had looked after Dawn on my first stint in hospital who had remained in touch and I now counted as one of my few friends).

The roads were clear and wide and I had a brilliant time until, without warning, I hit the rails at a level-crossing gate, obviously driving much too fast, but I really hadn't appreciated the speed I was doing. I skidded badly and crashed into the metal pillars to the side of the gates!

My, or should I say more accurately, Alan's beautiful pillar-box red, gleaming new car now looked like something ready to be taken to the scrap heap. It had a crumpled bonnet, front wing and door.

I experienced mounting panic at the knowledge that Alan was due back imminently, no doubt looking forward to getting behind the wheel of his new toy; like many men, his love affair with his car seemed to take precedence over everything—certainly me. I was in rather a dilemma— not least because I didn't have a driving license and I thought the long arm of the law might drive by at any moment which would be quite embarrassing to explain to Alan…

Someone answered my prayers; it was at least driveable and I sneaked the car back home. I borrowed some money from my wonderful friend and used all my feminine wiles (I had been a late starter in developing these talents, probably not surprisingly given my history, and they had crept up on me almost without my knowledge) to get a garage to undertake the work on an emergency basis. I had to confess all of course to the garage (just omitting the fact of not having a license!) and they thought it highly amusing. They entered into the spirit of the duplicity and actually returned the car, the paint still wet at four p.m. on the day Alan returned a few hours later!

I never told him and for all the years we kept the car, Alan used to, fairly regularly and certainly to my discomfort, say things like, 'I'm sure this car has had a bang, so-and-so is a slightly different shade,' and I would tell him not to be so neurotic. If he ever reads this book he will realise that his intuition was right after all.

I lost my neighbour, which I was sad about because she was helpful and friendly, but another took her place who proved to be someone who would have a great influence on my life. Her name was Ella.

As I got to know her, I found her to be a great friend. In her late forties or early fifties, really of indiscriminate age, very clever and bright, elegant and with the most amazing sense of humour, she had never married, but had several very discreet gentleman friends in high places and a philosophy of life which was to rub off on me.

I think for a while she was really my mentor as well as being my friend and I owe her a great deal; she taught me so much about life. But at the onset of our friendship I was merely a young mum, trying her best in the difficult circumstances of enforced separation to be a good, loving wife—to make my marriage work. Alan and the girls had turned my world around for me and I wanted to be the most important thing in their lives for them.

# –THIRTY–
# BETRAYAL

Alan returned from Rotterdam and once again started working locally. I was more than happy with my lot.

Isn't it funny how out of the blue, something can happen to change all that? In this case, a letter.

It came for Alan whilst he was at work. I had (with him being away most of the time) been used to opening all the mail and, indeed, with dealing with all the bills and expenses. Alan was not interested in doing anything connected with the day-to-day running of our household. I had rapidly taken this on board, and so on this ordinary day, I did what I always did without a thought as I slit open the envelope…

It was a love letter from a girl working in a bank in Rotterdam, just stating how much she was missing him.

From the contents of the letter it appeared she knew him intimately and there could have been no doubt they were sleeping together. I must have been incredibly naïve, but I can honestly say that it just wouldn't have occurred to me in a million years or in my wildest dreams that he would see someone else.

I had gone through the loneliness of bringing my first baby into the world on my own and carried the burden of worry about our little premature daughter entirely on my young shoulders whilst he was working away and yet I just trusted him implicitly.

Now trust was in tatters, and it just showed how little value he actually placed on our marriage.

I had never loved Alan but I was deeply fond of him and had the greatest respect. He had after all given me the most priceless gift, the means of keeping my beloved daughter in the desperate situation I had found myself in, showing a way towards the light at the end of my tunnel of despair. Now that respect was vanishing out of the window, so what was there left? If you love someone it is said that you can forgive him or her anything and that is probably true, but when that emotion isn't present in the deepest sense of the word there is a big void. My trust was violated.

Never one to cope with confrontation, I summoned up all my courage and when he returned asked him about the letter-writer.

He was almost whimsical, said it didn't mean a thing…these things happen and I shouldn't have opened his letter, then I wouldn't have been any the wiser. He wasn't apologetic, almost dismissive really and had a total disregard, or possibly, knowing Alan, ignorance of the hurt he had caused me.

I confided the hurt and rejection I was feeling to Ella next door. She wasn't a great fan of Alan, although to be fair she hardly knew him, but she disliked the fact that he placed so much on my shoulders, not really taking on board the practical responsibilities of having a family. Materialistically, he was kind and generous and never begrudged us anything and in that respect we were very lucky. Now she was angry for my sake, there with a shoulder to cry on, but she was quick to reaffirm her own sentiments about men—that was to enjoy what was on offer, never to get hurt and always to hold the upper hand and be in control. She certainly had the courage of her own convictions.

She was always boosting my confidence, telling me that I was a lovely young woman that most men would desire and that I should go through life using those attributes to benefit my own ends. I guess it was a 'Here ended the first lesson in overcoming adversity and finding myself' scenario, although I didn't want to hear it, feeling very sorry for myself, betrayed.

My self-esteem at that time was tumbling again in a downward spiral. I had tried so very hard to build on my relationship with Alan, and had thought we were succeeding, that our relationship was strengthening all the time, and that we had a mutual respect for each other. Now the letter had shown me that this obviously was not the case. I would certainly not have considered myself beautiful or desirable, very far from it, but Ella worked patiently with me, boosting my confidence, regaling me with tales of her friends—some very risqué, which had me in stitches—and passing on her zest for living.

He was working away again, no surprise there, but the trust had disappeared on my part; he was obviously living the life of a single person whilst away from us. Now I questioned his lack of communication during these contracts, whereas before I had put it down to a lack of enthusiasm for letter-writing; perhaps he was just too busy...

Ella was very instrumental in helping me to examine my innermost thoughts and my aspirations for the future. As young as I was and in spite of all the anguish of my past, reality hit that Alan really was not a part of my future but for the sake of my babies I wouldn't 'rock the boat', knowing from first-hand how much security was important to them.

I did make the decision though that I would live my own life provided that it in no way rubbed off on them. I would make the most of the opportunities that presented themselves to me.

I didn't realise it at that moment, but the seeds were being set for me to become a very ambitious, strong young lady. A butterfly emerging from the chrysalis!

# —THIRTY-ONE—
# 'FRIENDS'

Inevitable then that I would take a lover. If Alan didn't want me and all that! I was just vulnerable, needing someone to love me. He was a friend of Ella's. I had met him at a dinner party Ella gave. She entertained a lot and had loads of friends whom she plied with good food, witty conversation and excellent company.

It took me such a long to time to pluck up the courage to join one of her parties, although she always asked, anxious for me to get away from my own company. I just didn't have enough confidence in myself to meet and talk with other people outside of my immediate small circle of friends and acquaintances. Several times, I had got ready, but my nerve failed me at the last moment.

He was something in business, a very polite, nondescript sort of man that you would pass in the street without even so much as a glance, but intelligent, humorous, worldly and, quite beyond my comprehension, interested in me. (Two babies and a hectic lifestyle meant I didn't spend much time looking in the mirror and didn't take on board what was looking back at me anyway!)

Alan was abroad again, working—no surprise there. He didn't communicate; his affair had not been discussed after that initial confrontation. It was as if he felt it was nothing to do with me and that little word 'sorry', which might have made a small inroad into some reparation, certainly didn't feature. I was shutting myself off from him; he had caused me so much hurt and I had vowed that no one would do that to me again.

He, my new admirer, took me out for dinner on several occasions and seemed genuinely interested in me, regularly rang me, was utterly besotted, doing marvels for my morale and after a few weeks he made his move.

I can't pretend that I felt guilt or remorse at being unfaithful, it just seemed right somehow. Here was someone who valued me as a person, was as interested in my mind and my companionship as well as my body, something which was very lacking in my relationship with Alan.

Ironically, David (for that was his name) and I, in the several years we continued a friendship never actually made love in the truest sense of the word. The poor man suffered from premature ejaculation—I believe that is the term.

However, what he suffered in limitations in this quarter were more than compensated for in his prowess in bringing pleasure to his partner and the realisation hit me, as I blossomed under his skilful techniques that, until that moment, I had had no appreciation of what true fulfilment in sex had been about. In fact, my limited experiences with Alan, Kip too, had led me to believe that the whole thing was vastly overrated, a male pleasure thing. Now I knew differently!

Thank you, David!

Alan and I lived in a surreal world really; he worked away most of the time and was more like a fond uncle to the girls than a dad. As much as he loved them, he played no part in their upbringing, thinking it enough to ply them with gifts each time he returned. He was very generous and kindly though, and it didn't worry me to overlook his shortcomings, particularly as I was coming to terms with my own femininity and developing my own personality too.

By now I had taken a second driving test. Because I had driven myself around in the Mini when Alan wasn't around (he didn't know of course), it meant that I had picked up too many bad habits and drove far too cockily and probably badly.

The examiner hung on to his seat and got greyer by the moment.

I had borrowed a Mini for the occasion (and wore one too!) from someone in the village; it turned out to have a leaking petrol tank and no indicators either. I kept forgetting to do hand signals and the stench was terrible.

At the end of the practical test he told me that I had the most awful habit of cutting corners, was far too cocksure and so, just when I thought, 'Oh well this is it,' and that all the eyelash-fluttering and mini-skirted legs had been completely in vain, he concluded that as I obviously had the confidence to handle my car, even in a crisis situation, he was passing me.

He even managed a smile when I threw my arms around

his neck and kissed him. Perhaps it was just the sheer relief that he was back at the test centre in one piece!

Alan was involved in a project to do with the Mancunian Way, a new mammoth motorway project, and away for three or four weeks at the time, so I decided to pay him a surprise visit, travelling on a green-line coach up the motorway with my babies contentedly sleeping away the hours in the back.

He wasn't particularly pleased to see me, although he was working extremely hard on a night shift; but booked me into his hotel with the rejoinder that it was definitely only to be for two or three nights...

(Alan was the sort of man who just couldn't handle more than one thing at a time, as I was to realise over the years, he needed a hundred and one per cent to do his job which probably explained why he never wrote or even rang whilst he was away.)

But if his welcome was less than warm, I certainly had a memorable time!

The place was jam-packed full of dishy sun-tanned construction workers. No wonder the Diet Coke ads are so successful...we reach for the coke bottle to cool down our ardour! Squeezed into tight-fitting jeans, all with a twinkle in their eye and a healthy competition amongst themselves for a pretty face, I was in my element. In my newly awakened sensuality, I was fighting them off, but not very hard! Alan was oblivious to it.

One in particular, tenacious in his attentions, flirting through long sultry lashes, his body language causing my senses to lurch deliciously in a way I had forgotten since Kip, even when Alan was around, which somehow made it even more exciting, won my heart and we enjoyed unbridled nights of passion when Alan left to go to work.

He was hastily vacating the warmth of my bed only minutes before Alan returned to tumble wearily into it, after a hard night working. The danger aspect of being caught all added to the thrills of the moment. But I needn't have worried; he was obviously far too wrapped up in his job to notice that I was a hundredfold more exhausted when I got out of bed than when I got into it.

If I could have extended my stay I would have done. The delights of meandering around wonderful shops in the daytime (in the rural area where I lived, Charlie's shop was not a good comparison!) and enjoying illicit sexual romps at night, knew no bounds, but unfortunately Alan was having none of it and packed us off home.

I've just had a thought; maybe he was doing an imitation of the Diet Coke ad too, with someone else's wife, which was why he wanted rid of me. Who knows!

I didn't feel any contrition whatsoever. Had Alan respected our relationship I would have remained loyal and, yes, completely faithful to him; it wouldn't have occurred to me to do anything else. I suppose what it boiled down to at the end of the day was the desperate 'need' to be loved by someone.

It was something that I had tried to grasp all my life without ever really feeling I had attained it, and indeed would continue to do so for a great number of years yet.

Alan had hurt me dreadfully, and, in my immaturity, it didn't matter that I was seeking solace in what was certainly a four-letter word beginning with L, but Lust rather than Love.

## –THIRTY-TWO–
# The Visit

I was still seeking that Love word, not only for myself but now for my two little girls too—I desperately wanted a family unit for them. Of course, they had a grandma on Alan's side and aunts and uncles but because he was away all of the time, apart from the odd phone call to them when Alan was at home, we really had very little contact. Then, out of the blue, I must have had a brainstorm because I took my babies to see Dad and his family at their home in Kent.

This was a first for me; they never got in touch with me and infrequently I plucked up the courage and phoned. The response was never very warm, but I was a glutton for punishment, always with hope in my heart that things might change for the better—and perhaps I just wanted them to see I had overcome the worst of what they had done to me.

Apart from the time Dad had paid a visit just after Dawn was born I hadn't seen hair nor hide and, apart from a rare few words always instigated by me on the phone, there had been no contact. He had not even seen Debbie nor acknowledged her birth.

Knowing that WW no longer lived with them, I reasoned that Alice could only be a better person for her departure and I really wanted my sister and brother to meet their nieces too and find some love in their hearts for them. How could they not? In my heart of hearts I longed for there to be some for me too.

I was deluding myself...

I had reasoned that I was my own person now, would be able to cope with rejection, safe in the knowledge that I could take my precious cargo with me and be away if things didn't go as they should. Of course what I really wanted was for them to open their arms to my babies and me and envelop us in the warmth of a real family.

Some hope.

The visit was not a success; we were neither welcomed nor enriched by the experience.

I was pleased to see my sister and brother after such a long while of course, but Alice could not resist belittling my parenting skills, taking every opportunity to criticise and make derisory comments to undermine my confidence.

Dad, clearly uncomfortable, said nothing.

In fact I was an excellent little mum: my girls were happy and the epitome of contentment, knowing only warmth and love in their home environment but it was amazing that, after only a few short hours, my self-esteem had fallen again to zero and I questioned whether I was indeed capable of bringing them up properly.

In such a cold unwelcoming environment, I could see

no option but to turn tail and come home, undertaking the long rail and bus journeys once again. If they were concerned at the stamina this would take out of us, they certainly didn't express it, and although my father did run us to the station, Alice didn't even bother to say goodbye. It had taken hours to get there and we were on our way back home again in what seemed like minutes. There was no train for well over an hour but it was preferable to wait on that anonymous station platform than in the unwelcome arena of Alice's home.

And once again (and I've lost count of the amount of times I uttered those words in my lifetime) I vowed 'never again'.

## -THIRTY-THREE-
## FAMILY LINKS

However, sometimes life compensates and out of the blue the lack of grandparental love my girls were missing out on was more than compensated for from another quarter and it seemed for the first time since the death of my beloved Louise, I once again had a real family of my own.

You will recall Alan's stepbrother, his wife and family. They began to take on the role almost of surrogate parents/grandparents, visiting us often, and they showered my little girls with affection. They spoilt them and, indeed me, rotten and in my wildest dreams I couldn't have asked for more.

Their children treated me like a sibling (they were a similar age to me and a happy, caring family, more than willing to welcome me into their midst) and I allowed myself for the first time to lower my guard and develop a camaraderie with them which for so long had been missing in my life.

Terry and Eileen were like the parents I hadn't had and I couldn't have wished for better. I was so happy, perhaps more fulfilled than I had ever been in my life.

When Jackie, their daughter, got married from home, I was as excited to help with the wedding preparations as if it was my own wedding. My cup really ran over with joy. It didn't matter that Alan was away most of the time, it really felt that it was my little girls and I who were so important in their lives and I felt so lucky to be given this love to help me heal the scars.

It was short-lived.

To this day I still haven't the least idea what transpired although I have drawn my own conclusions (see Author's Notes, page 216).

Completely out of the blue, Terry telephoned me (nothing unusual in this as one or other of the family called most days for a natter). But this was a sombre Terry, very far from his usual jovial self. He told me that—as absurd as it may seem—Eileen had decided that he was having an affair with me and that they wouldn't be visiting any more. At first I thought it was a wind-up, a sick joke, but it was very real.

What could have put such a weird idea in her head I just would never know?

Terry and Eileen represented parent figures in my life and Terry and I had only ever experienced the sort of light-hearted banter that takes place between fathers and daughters; it wouldn't have occurred to either of us in a million years for it to be anything else.

I was completely devastated, heartbroken.

What was even more upsetting to me though was that,

for whatever reason Eileen had conceived this idea, her own children, with whom I'd got on so well, hadn't stepped in to reassure her as to how absurd the whole thing was. I never heard a peep from them.

I suppose, with hindsight, the only saving grace was that my girls had been too small to remember this brief interlude in their lives when they had enjoyed the love of surrogate grandparents, albeit temporarily.

I never saw or heard from them again from that day.

Whatever had happened in Eileen's life to cause her to draw such a totally illogical conclusion remains a mystery but they did me a very great wrong and I just hope that no one gives them the sort of anguish that their actions gave me.

## – THIRTY-FOUR –
## NEW HORIZONS

We moved house: the farm wanted the cottage for an estate worker which took precedence and we decided we would look to buy our own starter home. I was very sad, most of all at leaving my beloved Ella who had done so very much to help me build up my self-esteem—she was such a good friend—but also leaving the peace and tranquillity of the countryside around about. My babies couldn't have had more idyllic surroundings in which to thrive and it was my sanctuary.

But there was also excitement at starting anew to make friendships with younger people in similar circumstances to myself with young families. This had been missing, unfortunately, from where we were living as the village housed mostly older people and, as kind as they were, it was not quite the same.

Alan was quite content to leave it all to me. Choosing

the house, the area, and even arranging the mortgage—as was always the pattern in our lives, he went along with it amicably enough provided it didn't disrupt his lifestyle too much or call for input from him.

It heralded the start of one of the happiest times of my entire life. I cemented friendships that would see me through probably the rest of my life. We were all in a similar boat with small children, not a lot of money although most of them had their partners around.

I was valued for the first time as a person, as a good mum, and my organisational skills were put to the test in helping to set up a playgroup. Of course I was a baby by comparison to most of my peers in similar circumstances at nineteen/twenty but I kept my extreme youth to myself and I think all of my friends assumed I was a few years older. I certainly had an old head on young shoulders.

I didn't disillusion them!

Alan as always was away but I had a good friend, Joyce, whose husband was also away working so we kept each other company in the evenings too. My house was always full of people and laughter and if I was lonely I shut my mind to it.

Inevitably, affairs and gossip were rife as in any estate-type environment and it would have been an unusual day if some of the same weren't exchanged over morning coffee or a natter over the fence.

My next-door neighbour was a likeable rogue; a greeting-card salesman with an eye for a pretty face, known, it would seem, to everyone except his wife. It appeared he was incapable of keeping his flies done up and my life was blighted with unexpected visits when he catapulted over the fence seeking sanctuary from the latest irate husband, when he would grovel and plead for me to keep his wife occupied whilst he dealt with the situation—usually this meant legging it through my back door!

The worst occasion was when someone attacked his front door with an axe. His wife was fortunately away at a WI meeting at the time, and remained blissfully unaware, although it cost him dearly for my silence on that occasion! (He was doing my household chores for weeks!)

On my part I was still seeing David on occasion, which, as he was completely besotted, served to boost my ego, if nothing else.

I flirted when the occasion arose and had the occasional fling when the fancy took me, but on the whole I was content with my life as it was.

As well as a varied assortment of wonderful female friends in those days, I also had a friend whom I probably valued as much if not more than any of them. His name was Roger and he was the site agent on the housing development—a job probably not suited to his temperament one iota. He was a Welshman to the core; quick-tongued, didn't tolerate fools easily and had a wicked sense of humour.

He spent many hours with me, probably because he hated his job so much, and we would put the world to rights together.

Inevitably, there was speculation, because of the sheer amount of time we spent in each other's company, that we were having a relationship and, given his humour and sense of fun, he loved to fuel it in any way he could.

I remember one New Year's Eve when he and his wife

were holding a party to which I had been invited. Towards the end of the evening, he insisted that he accompany me home to 'help me get my boots off'! This of course caused a few raised eyebrows, deliberately provoked by him and I (unlike him) was totally embarrassed as we came away.

In truth that was exactly what he was doing… . I had purchased a pair of, at that time, highly fashionable vinyl-type high boots, in which I was utterly incapable of moving even an inch to get the wretched things off. It was as though they were super-glued to my skin and as I got hotter and thus sweatier, it got worse!

Roger and I rolled round the floor for a good half an hour in various contortions which would have done a sex manual justice (and would certainly have added fuel to the gossip if anyone had peered through the windows and I wouldn't have put it past them!), as we tried to get to grips with the wretched things. Eventually, in total desperation, we resorted to a pair of scissors, laughing so much that we nearly had convulsions and we both felt it was the best entertainment of the evening.

This was the first and, as they now lay in tatters, only time I wore them. What we girls do in the name of vanity!

Mission accomplished, he wandered home.

I often wondered what his wife Janet—a lovely person and someone I have been proud to call a friend all these years—felt, although I'm sure she loved and trusted him enough to realise the truth. Yes, we were indeed having a relationship, but not of a sexual nature. We were just the greatest chums; he helped me to value myself and to foster my ambitions, putting yet another piece into place in the jigsaw that was my attempt to learn to value myself as a person. Roger was one of the few people I had used as a confidante, letting him into my world of rejection, giving him an insight into my life; he with his great sense of humour was instrumental in helping me place things in perspective, and I was lucky enough to count him one of my closest friends.

Of course he quickly moved on to areas which were much more suited to his skills and indeed intelligence and I saw much less of him; after a while, he and Janet moved and made their home elsewhere.

Notwithstanding, we always kept in touch and I felt a terrible sense of loss to hear that he was suffering from cancer and, in spite of his determination to fight it, lost the battle and died prematurely in his forties.

I have no doubt whatsoever that someone somewhere is benefiting from his sense of humour and, who knows, maybe he is helping one of the angels up there put her boots on too (what's the betting, they're white vinyl!).

# Thirty-Five
# Temper Tantrums

Alan came home on occasion; sadly he didn't mix very much with my new circle of friends. He was always polite but kept a distance; he was ill at ease, for we really had very little in common other than the girls, but, in his own way, I guess he was happy enough with his lot. He had more of a life away from us than with us.

Although most of the time a very placid person, he had a vile temper, which, if aroused, I felt, would mean he wouldn't be responsible for his actions.

On one of the rare occasions we had ever talked in depth (our relationship just wasn't like that, it was superficial really), I had stated that, if ever he hit me, I would leave him. I had never talked to Alan about the nightmare that had been my life, the violence and the far-reaching effect it had had on me, the aftermath of which would remain with me for always. Not surprisingly, I felt that any form of aggression, in whatever form it took, if it occurred again, would be a breaking point for me.

I hadn't experienced violence from Alan I must quickly add, but his mother had regaled me with tales of incidents where he had been violent towards other people, and thus, with my memories of past abuse just below my mind's surface, I had felt I needed the reassurance from making this stipulation.

I never expected to act upon it.

On a rare home visit, Alan had completely without thinking, unplugged the freezer switch to use his electric razor, forgetting to replace it overnight. Things like that happen to everyone at some time or another, I am sure.

Everything was completely defrosted—there was a river of ice cream, melted mousses, and so on winding its way across the floor, and everything else was in sodden packaging immersed in water! But, in this instance, the 'everything' belonged to my friend across the road—Joyce, whose own freezer had become defunct and I had suggested she use mine whilst awaiting delivery of a new one.

Now Joyce was someone who commanded a healthy respect; she was very meticulous about her routines and behaviour and, if truth were known, I was more than a little afraid and in awe of her. With her sharp Scottish tongue when things didn't go her way, she was more than a force to be reckoned with! An Auntie Nell Mark 11.

She was very critical of some of my scattier friends and I was always on my best behaviour with her, never quite spontaneous. Her husband worked away too, something to do with 'the secret service' or more accurately, the Diplomatic Core, which all sounded very high-flying. As we were both on our own, I spent a lot of time with her and I suppose I (with my lack of confidence) was a little bemused that she wanted to be 'my' friend.

So facing this slush mountain of defrosted food, I was hysterical. I think if truth were known, it was not so much because of what had happened, but the prospect of having to confess all to Joyce. She would most definitely not be amused! I toyed with the idea of refreezing it all but most of it was ice-cream and items beyond redemption that I couldn't dust off and pretend were all right.

I shouted at Alan in terms which could almost have been reminiscent of Alice's heyday and he in return, became very angry (for which he was probably quite justified!), losing his temper completely and giving me a couple of resounding slaps across the face. I probably was hysterical but this *was* the first time we had ever had a physical confrontation. (I tried to bite his hand too as he hit me, a throw-back to the physical onslaughts from Alice and the need to protect myself.) Galvanised into action by the sheer shock of this, I, totally irrationally said I was leaving—well, perhaps not so irrationally, as I reasoned he would have to be the one to confess all to Joyce!

I hastily packed an overflowing bag and, with my two bemused daughters in tow, along with one oversized double pushchair in the pouring rain, tried to make a dignified exit over unmade up muddy roads with a reluctant dog dragging behind me, belongings dropping out here, there and everywhere as I pushed and pummelled my way. I must have looked a comical sight.

I really was making a mountain out of a molehill but it somehow didn't seem like that.

I didn't have a clue where I was going or, where for that matter, I could go. And here I believe with all my heart that destiny, my karma, was responsible for my actions on that day, not any spontaneity on my part. I had hardly any money with me; my behaviour was really to teach Alan a lesson, and to avoid Joyce's wrath although I wasn't admitting that to myself!

I walked a couple of miles down the A5 to the local garage, trying to gather my thoughts. I didn't want to lose face with Alan by going straight back (there was no way I planned for it to be anything other than a very temporary arrangement though). The proprietor was a guy called Derek; I'd met up with him once or twice when I'd gone with friends to get petrol.

Seeing I was upset, he offered to drive me somewhere but I couldn't think where to say, that wasn't miles and miles away and I don't think he'd have been too impressed that I only had a fiver with me either!

To this day I don't have a clue why, standing there in the pouring rain, with grizzling children and whining dog, mud-splattered, sodden hair dripping down my face, I asked him to take me to Dad's (& Alice's). Perhaps the slaps across the face had affected my brain! I don't know, it was totally illogical. Looking back at it now, I really do think it was some sort of divine intervention, twist of fate somewhere directing me there, but at the time I put it down to the fact that I must have lost some of my brain cells with the unexpected slaps.

This wasn't to Kent, incidentally; even I wasn't that potty; they had very recently moved from Kent into Oxfordshire as Dad was taking on a very big, new project somewhere.

He had sent a change-of-address card with this brief explanation on it and the place they had moved to would seem to be only a reasonably short drive from where we were, certainly under an hour's driving distance.

Derek agreed but didn't look too happy at the pushchair encased in a foot of mud on its wheels and a bedraggled dog to boot. He would have been even less impressed if he had realised I didn't have any money! What a pretty face can do! But not so pretty at that moment, I must have looked like Orphan Annie!

Less than an hour later, we pulled up at the door of this nondescript house, whilst I tried to make a dignified exit from the car, promising Derek to pay him for his unofficial taxi in the very near future.

With one hand wrestling with the holdall, the other with the dog, and my heel barely touching the kerb from the open car door, the front door of the house was flung open to display Alice shouting at the top of her voice, 'My God she's left him; what if he won't take her back?'

'What do you want here?'

Nothing like a warm welcome! Thank God it wasn't a serious emergency!

## —THIRTY-SIX—
## FATE

I shepherded my girls into the house, explaining that it was only temporary, overnight, and that Alan would be picking me up later.

I didn't offer an explanation and they certainly weren't looking for one. They were obviously horrified. My priority was to settle the girls who were obviously confused. After all, these people were strangers to them.

I rang the site office on the estate (we didn't have a phone of our own) and asked them to put a note through our door asking Alan to pick me up ASAP. This had been a terrible mistake…sanity was very quick to return.

Early afternoon turned into evening and he didn't show up. We sat in stony silence; at least the girls had a good time playing with my sister, but if looks could kill I would have been buried, never mind dead. Night-time, the girls and I snuggled into a single bed, but sleep didn't come to me. I sneaked into the garage and fetched Ja Ja in.

Here I was in the most unlikely spot, the most unwelcoming situation. What had sent me here?

Morning came, the atmosphere was even worse. A knock at the door: my initial relief when I thought it was Alan turned into surprise that it was in fact Alice's GP making a house call on a Sunday with no one ill. Although I was not specifically invited to be a part of the conversation, I couldn't fail to catch the gist. Namely, that whilst in Kent—and we were talking of a period well in excess of twelve months before this—Alice had had a cervical smear done privately through a ladies' clinic as she had been too embarrassed to go to her male GP for issues of a personal nature Somehow, her records had been mislaid, not linked back to her GP and it had taken all this time to trace her and indeed get back to her with the results.

It was positive.

I witnessed my father's face drain to an ashen grey. Was this history repeating itself? Elizabeth and David were only small children, younger by far than I was when Louise had died.

Arrangements were made for Alice to undergo tests on an emergency basis with a view to immediate hospitalisation. The quandary about me turning up on the doorstep was eclipsed by the trauma of the moment and so it came about that, when Alan turned up to collect me we had to squeeze in two extra passengers, for Elizabeth and David came back with me. And there was no time for repercussions.

It certainly wasn't Alice's choice. She couldn't bear to breathe the same air as me, let alone trust her children to my care, but in this instance, her wishes were, I think, overruled by my father.

He was always one to opt for the easiest option and there wasn't anyone else to care for them, short of them going temporarily into care.

Had I not, by this weird twist of fate, been on the spot I am sure that the latter option would have been preferable to Alice rather than ask me, but I was.

Whilst there was certainly no love in my feelings for Alice, it was almost too much to bear for me to contemplate that she too might be taken away from her children; although I'd had so very little to do with them, I loved them dearly.

Not surprisingly, she was absolutely terrified; perhaps in shock himself, Dad seemed incapable of offering her physical comfort and so (probably quite illogically but there you go) I wanted to reach out and comfort her, to cradle this distraught woman in my arms and offer her what solace I could. I wanted to reassure her that her children would be loved and cared for and in that moment of compassion, the defences were temporarily abandoned and I rocked her tightly against my body, soothing, reassuring her. Again, I had an old head on a young body and for a fleeting moment, all the animosity she felt towards me was forgotten as she searched for comfort.

The victim was offering solace to the perpetrator.

Elizabeth and David became part of my family for quite a few weeks.

Alice had emergency treatment culminating in a hysterectomy and there was the recuperation period when she wasn't strong enough to cope with the children and needed to convalesce. It was a lovely time for me to get to know my sister and brother whom I just hadn't had the opportunity to know before.

For them too, I hoped they'd realise that their sister or whatever they were told I was, wasn't the ogre she had been considered to be and we were a happy little bunch.

Eventually they went back home. Given the circumstances and the time delays in Alice commencing treatment, they were exceedingly lucky to still have a mum to return to, but, unlike me, fate had been kinder to them.

Had this not been the case though, I was determined that they would never know the loneliness and unhappiness that had been a part of my life in similar circumstances and would have fought tooth and nail to protect them and keep them as part of my family too.

I was probably naïve to feel that, in recognition of my help, Alice might, when recovered, mellow towards me and welcome me more into the family (for this was all I had ever wanted really). Yet the reality was that I had encroached upon 'her' family, no matter what the circumstances, they now had fond memories of me, and her jealousy and resentment escalated to an even higher level.

## -THIRTY-SEVEN-
## STORKS STIRRING

Maybe to eclipse the hurt of this happening—I don't know, but probably not for the right reasons, I felt that I would really like another baby, a little boy if possible, although you can't choose of course. Yet my instincts told me it would be.

Alan, as always, was amenable as long as it didn't directly affect him. Ours was a strange relationship really, and it was as though he was on the peripheral of family life, not unhappy, but just not going anywhere.

I made my own life; my own plans and he did likewise. Strangely perhaps, I never questioned what he did or didn't do in his personal life away from home. Our physical relationship consisted of occasional sex, no warmth or loving, but it seemed to be working.

I was fulfilled enough in my lifestyle at that time not to have needed further relationships. I had had one or two brief flings not even worthy of mention really, and David and I had gone our different ways mutually.

This would be the first planned baby for me and I wanted it to be born at home, surrounded by my girls, friends and neighbours.

For someone that had had so little love and warmth in my life for so long, I valued those relationships and the lifestyle I enjoyed so much now, that there couldn't have been a better time.

I was lucky that I conceived straight away, having a healthy and happy pregnancy.

I had acquired a little Mini Clubman which my friend Derek at the garage (yes, I had repaid his impromptu taxi!) sprayed a bright pea green for me and I was as happy as Larry bombing here there and everywhere.

I was also extremely lucky that I had a lovely GP who had recently joined our local surgery and my baby was to be his first home delivery here, which he was enthusiastic about.

The existing doctor in the practice was something else; a very imposing, elderly gentleman, of indiscriminate age but definitely seventy going on a hundred and seventy. His surgery was like something out of a past decade. You stood in a room, dimly lit, panelled with dark oak, a counter running across the middle at least four or five feet in height. On the other side would stand Dr Reid, only his bald head clearly visible, whilst he questioned what was wrong with you. It would take a brave soul to be a malingerer here! You almost expected his hand to shoot up and disinfectant spray to hit the air!

He was an excellent doctor but talk about intimidating you!

In theory he was retiring and thus the new GP, Dr Rankin, was taking over his practice. In practical terms, however, this was a long way off as Dr Reid was very reluctant to let go the reins.

The baby was due in the middle of July. The date came and went, everyone, midwife, doctor, said I was going to have the baby imminently but nothing happened. Dr Rankin, knowing how much I wanted a home delivery, tried to do a sweep (I believe that is separating the neck of the womb from the membranes to agitate labour) but without success.

The 30th July saw my Dawn's fifth birthday party. I had promised her a baby brother. What better present?

At its height, Dr Reid arrived on the doorstep.

Grabbing a piece of cake, in his usual inimitable style he suggested that I 'get your knickers off gal, let's take a look at you'! as if he was asking for a cup of tea, and here followed yet another examination, but here was someone with a wealth of experience behind him whose opinion was law, enforcing the sentiments of Dr Rankin and the midwife, that I was going to have the baby at any moment. Grabbing a handful of goodies on his way out, he left as quickly as he had come.

However, a few more days went by with absolutely nothing happening, I was pretty peed off by this time so Dr Rankin reluctantly (purely because of the disappointment on my part for wanting this baby to be born at home with my family) decided that I would have to visit the hospital, promising me faithfully that I could return home the minute the baby was born if I wanted to!

I packed a bag, although Dr Rankin, being unfamiliar with the obstetric admission routine in this area, sent me through the channels of the normal antenatal clinic, rather than what was customary, in the case of induction, straight to the ward. Thus I had to go through the entire rigmarole for a new patient—blood tests, screening, urine tests and so on, with everyone looked pretty shocked in response to the 'when is your baby due?' question...'three weeks ago actually'. By the time I eventually saw a consultant, I was weary, fed up to the high teeth with lugging a great big bag around with me from department to department. He voiced the inevitable cliché...'You're going to have this baby at any moment, come back on Monday [it was Friday] if nothing's happened.' I'd had enough, rebellion set in!

I plonked myself on my bag, not the best of moves given my extended abdomen, stating with weary determination that I had been told this by everyone for well over a week; I wasn't leaving the hospital without a baby, thank you very much, enough was enough! I don't know where I got my dogmatism from but I surely meant it!

For a fleeting moment I think he was going to argue, but it was the end of clinic on a busy Friday afternoon and I was probably the last straw between him and a cup of tea or maybe even a G&T! He expelled a big sigh of resignation, and asked the nurses to find me a bed somewhere. I think, looking at my determined face, this was the easy option, and allowed the poor man to depart, no doubt to regale his friends at the dinner table of this stroppy woman who refused to budge!!

I'd left my girls in the capable hands of a good friend

and Alan was due home too to take control so I had no worries.

Later that evening, my waters were broken and I came into labour, within seconds giving birth to my son speedily within a couple of hours.

He's always been a lazy little bugger, needing a foot up his backside to get him moving, so what's new!

It was disturbing that the placenta had started to decompose due to him being so overdue and the midwives were all very concerned about this as obviously be could have been starved of nutrients, but he seemed fit and healthy and at eight pounds-something, a monster by comparison to my girls.

My joy was complete and I was already making plans to go home first thing in the morning.

# —THIRTY-EIGHT—
# FEARS

Come the morning, my little boy, Ian, was very jaundiced and the hospital, although not then overly concerned, felt it was best that we stay put and pump extra fluids into him.

One day merged into two, two into three, the Rubin tests were quite high, the jaundice didn't abate. I was desperate to get home, missing my girls; I had so much wanted this to be a family event.

At that time, children weren't allowed in the hospital and I had to be content with holding Ian up to the window for two little faces to try and get a glimpse of him from several floors below. So different from before, when I had been so alone, now I had so many kindly friends fighting over caring for my wee girls and I knew they would be spoilt rotten but I still couldn't bear to be away from them.

What came as a complete surprise was that Dad visited the hospital, seemingly making a great fuss about his 'first grandson'. I recalled he was euphoric about his son too when he was born. Must be something about the male genes. To other people in the ward he would have been judged a proud grandfather but only I knew better.

It was the first time he had ever spontaneously visited me and it seemed definitely like shutting the stable door after the horse has bolted and all that…I was secretly cross that Alan had even told him.

A week had gone by; I was tumbling into the pits of postnatal depression because I was so desperate to go home. I felt that the application of increased fluid levels—which was the only perceived treatment Ian was having—could be carried out just as successfully at home. He was still very jaundiced and the Billy Rubin Tests were still high. There was no irregularity with his blood group necessitating a blood transfusion, so other factors were being investigated.

I was at my wit's end.

Dr Rankin came to my rescue. He had been so kind, calling in to visit me on most days, knowing how homesick and disappointed I was. Now he took responsibility for me and my son and I was discharged into his care though needing to return in a few days for more blood tests.

There were heart-stopping words being mentioned here—leukaemia, blood disorders: I was distraught.

My homecoming was not as happy as it should have been with so much worry hanging over me, but people were so very kind and I had amassed over two hundred cards from well-wishers. I was completely humbled that people cared so much.

Ours was a lovely village where old and new inhabitants alike had mixed and been welcoming to each other and I knew most of them; now it seemed they wanted to show they were thinking about me. The house was like a flower shop and I was truly overwhelmed by the thoughtfulness of people. It's very true to say that you can't choose your family but you choose your friends and I couldn't have wished for better.

Dr Reid also showed his support in his gruff way, calling in to see me, reassuring me that he felt sure everything would be OK.

Ian returned to the hospital for more tests.

The blood tests he underwent, which were pretty gruesome for a tiny baby, showed that the platelets being released from the spleen were immaturely formed; this, it seemed, could be a hereditary condition or be linked to contact with radiation.

This in itself was terrifying because Alan's job involved X-Rays and on my side, being adopted, I could give no insight into family history; I just didn't know from where the problems emanated.

At least leukaemia was ruled out, but it seemed it would be likely, as soon as he was old enough to withstand the operation, that his spleen would need to be removed.

Like so many parents, I felt it so unfair that this should be happening to such a tiny baby, I wished I could take over the suffering for him.

But against all the odds, he did improve, the jaundice abated and this considered operation was put on hold... . Although closely monitored, we got him through his first birthday with his spleen still intact and his body seemed now to be in control of its irregular platelets and it was felt optimistically that he might outgrow the problem.

Thank you, God.

# —THIRTY-NINE—
# Dignity

I greatly valued the support I had from Dr Rankin; he always said (I believe he was fairly newly married and his wife too was a lovely person that I met on a couple of occasions) that, if he had a son half as good as Ian, he would be delighted. I hope he had many…

It is funny with us females though, how our dignity does a full circle before during and after a pregnancy, isn't it?

My doctor and I thankfully had a lovely camaraderie and throughout my pregnancy I could and did put up with anything, no matter how demoralising and reminiscent of a cattle market! Legs in stirrups, internal examinations—we take them all in our stride without batting an eyelid, but hold in there. Almost to the minute that umbilical cord is cut and—excluding the odd stitches of course!—your dignity returns and with it your decorum, I guess.

When I had my postnatal examination, Dr Rankin, with a nurse present, gave me my internal examination as is the norm and said, whilst in the midst of it, considering himself extremely witty, 'Hold on, I've just passed a double decker bus in here!!'

He thought it highly amusing. It was the sort of joke, which I would and did accept quite happily during my pregnancy with the excellent rapport we had, but I was completely mortified, bursting into tears.

I am sure the poor man must have thought I'd lost my marbles, but there you go, I've remembered it forever!

So, if a double decker bus ever goes missing, you know where 'not' to look!

# –FORTY–
# Contentment

I was so lucky with my friends, although it didn't quite make up for the lack of a spouse or partner around, particularly in those companionable hours of the evenings when the little ones were asleep. I found this to be the time when I didn't enjoy my own company and was envious of this happily filled space in my friends' lives. Still, I really knew the meaning of the words 'true friendship' with them around.

I certainly needed their support with Ian on the scene. He might have lost one of his nine lives at birth but he certainly lost the other eight too, in that first year or so.

He was a monster; accident-prone wasn't the word!

He managed to completely rock his pram over at eight months old, knocking out his two front teeth (which he hadn't had very long in the first place!) and if someone could fall out of a window, climb into a hole, shut himself in a cupboard, eat something definitely not fit for human consumption, you can bet your bottom dollar it would be Ian.

I had him on a bungee rope to the doctor's surgery; we had to visit so often after one mishap or another; I'm amazed he didn't go on to a Children at Risk register! But, typical of all little boys, with one of his endearing smiles, toothless as it now was, I could forgive him anything. He was certainly Mummy's boy and could wind me, and his sisters, around his little finger.

I busied myself in the evenings doing a job for a firm called Baby Showers to combat the loneliness; it was a sort of party plan company specialising in children's wear. Much of the time I just ran parties at home (although babysitters were always easy to find), and I enjoyed the company as well as making some money. The only trouble was that I liked the clothes so much I spent all the money I made on buying them but I certainly had well dressed children!

I was fulfilled as a mother but I still felt that I had a surplus of love to give. My marriage was totally unsatisfying and yet relationships with other people at the time didn't seem the answer either, I was—to all intents and purposes—a single-parent family and, practically, I needed to devote my time to my children.

I was only twenty-one. This milestone birthday had gone uncelebrated as most birthdays did. My friends all thought I was older and Alan as always was away. I did have a moment of sadness, but I wouldn't have known how to let my hair down anyway. I had never had a party since a small child and certainly not birthday gifts…I'd never been to a dance in my life and would most certainly have had two left feet, given my total lack of dexterity. I'd never even seen the inside of a night club—I suppose it's true to say what you don't have, you don't miss. I had my children and my friends, and was acutely aware that there was plenty of time for my life to take further directions when the time was right. I knew that I was ambitious and wanted much more in my life: a career; and someone who loved me as a person, to name but two, but the time wasn't then, and I wasn't ready to move forward, so, in the main, I was content with my lot.

# —FORTY-ONE—
# SHARING THE LOVE

We all need to be needed, to find vessels in which to channel our feelings and I was no exception.

I had so much love to give, I adored my children, yet I still had more; I decided to channel my energies and surplus affections into an area where it would be of the utmost use—fostering.

Of course it couldn't be a partnership venture with Alan away all the time and he wouldn't have wanted to be involved, so some types of fostering were not viable but Pre-Adoption Fostering was. It seemed it was no time at all before nappies; bottles and tiny babies dominated our household once again.

This was instigated through a Christian Adoption Agency and was usually for the first eight weeks or so directly following the birth of the babies, which was the period of time when natural mothers could make their final decisions governing their babies' futures, before signing adoption papers.

Some babies stayed much longer though—if they were in the care of a paediatrician following their birth, or their future wasn't quite so cut and dried and adoption wasn't the natural option.

Over a period of time, we probably had a dozen babies; they were all adorable, of course, and it was lovely to think we were instrumental in ensuring those first precious few weeks were full of security and love.

One that has an extra special place in my heart was a little girl, Sheryl, from a West Indian family. She remained with me for nearly a year. Mum had been terribly young and Grandma had been reluctant to allow her to go for adoption but was unable to care for her herself, so she stayed—spreading delight in my life—whilst the family visited religiously every week. Eventually she returned to her family, with them uniting to share the care. A happy outcome.

The mums and relatives were all welcome to visit, of course, and some did, but most didn't. The ones that did were inevitably tearful and visibly torn as to whether they were doing the right thing.

It was my job to provide a loving environment for their babies, to provide a warm, welcoming atmosphere for them if they chose to visit; not to make suggestions, there were excellent social workers for that, but it was strange for me—somehow I had come full circle.

My adopted parents had never told me the nature of my background, but I presumed I was a product of just such a situation; dealing with these special babies and their mums somehow brought the memories all flooding back.

On the one hand, I wished with all my heart that I had had my natural parents and then I might would have not been subjected to the sadness in my childhood, yet, on the other hand, no one could have loved me more than my adopted parents; they had wanted me so very much and Louise had always told me how extra special I was and that I was a chosen one… . No one could have loved and cherished me more than she did and even Dad too, at that time, before it all went pear-shaped.

The reality was that in truth, I was a victim of fate, of destiny. It could equally well have happened whoever I was with…

My heart went out to these young girls (ironically though many were probably older than me!) making decisions about their and their babies' futures; this was undoubtedly the hardest thing they would ever have to do in their lives. Whatever the outcome, they would have to live with it and it would remain in their thoughts forever.

There was one decision I made at this time and that was that, when the time was right—and I felt intuitively I would know when this was the case, perhaps when I was strong enough to face rejection, I'm not sure—I would attempt to trace my natural parents.

# —FORTY-TWO—
# C'EST LA VIE

Whilst concluding this book, the first, about my life as, first, child, then vulnerable teenager, which ultimately is a story of hope, of overcoming the most overwhelming diversity, of finding myself, it would seem entirely fitting to end with this final chapter about finding my identity, my roots.

The time span between the penultimate chapter and this final one is over ten years.

In the former, you leave a young lady, barely out of her teens with her young family, preparing to follow the paths that destiny mark out for her, good, bad, sad and happy.

You rejoin her, a confident young lady in her mid-thirties, successful, self-reliant and confident, for whom, she has decided, the time is right to try and trace her natural mother.

How I had come to this decision I'm not sure, for when, in one's heart of hearts can one ever be sure that the time is really right...? Yes, I was self-assured, confident, emotionally cherished and secure. I had a man in my life who was supportive and behind me one hundred per cent—not Alan of course—a loving family, and a lifestyle that many would envy. Never did I take that for granted; I was so lucky. I think that, collectively, they represented to me the knowledge that I was now strong enough to face rejection should it arise.

We all delude ourselves, don't we?

How many times did I rationalise that it wasn't that I wanted a mother...didn't need that relationship...? I just wanted to know my origins, my roots...!

There was someone out there from whom I had inherited my determination, my business acumen, my warmth, my character traits, warts and all; surely I had the right to have that knowledge?

Sure, tracing natural parents has been made an awful lot easier over the past few years. It had become a relatively easy process to obtain a copy of your natural birth certificate, have a brief chat with a social worker, take away a form to fill in, and away you go.

I was raring to go, the epitome of self-assurance, but deep down, in the very innermost depths of my mind, definitely not on show to anyone, lay that insecure little girl who very desperately needed to be loved.

So yes, I'll put my hand up and admit it: in spite of the bravado, the 'right' words, all I really wanted was a mum, and no, I don't think anyone, no matter how self-assured that person might be, can truly handle rejection.

The procedure is quite easy to get the ball rolling: I see a social worker, give out the right responses and she in return gives out the obligatory cautionary warnings. But we've been there, in the last paragraph, haven't we? We listen, but do we take on board? From here she completes the necessary forms with which I can gain a copy of my natural birth certificate.

So far, so good.

I had it, quite an innocuous document, a birth certificate; but the start of another chapter of my life

It seemed strange to know that I had in fact been called Carol Lyn (particularly as Louise's second name had been Carol).

I wasn't a Carol, most definitely a Sandie. Strangely too, my surname had been almost identical to that of my adoptive parents, just one letter different.

I experienced a surge of excitement when I noted my place of birth was Brockett Hall! I had always known I was related to the aristocracy, blue-blooded and all that!

I was swiftly brought down to earth, however, when I realised that the same place had been part of the City of Westminster Hospital at the end of the war! Oh well, we can all have our dreams, albeit fleetingly, can't we?

I knew that the hard work began here, starting to search the births, marriages and deaths registers at St Katherine's House.

I found what I thought was the marriage records for my mother some eighteen months or so after my birth, but try as I might I could find no birth records for her.

Whether the system has changed now, I have no idea, but then you completed a form, paid your fee and then had an interminable wait of ten days or so for the certificate to be posted to you. The information at your disposal in the ledgers from which you make your assumption that you have found the right entry, is very basic and to a certain degree it is a gamble. If it was wrong then you started the process all over again.

I was lucky; the certificate was the right one. The address was the same as on my birth certificate, in Surrey and her husband's address was also in the same vicinity.

I drew a complete blank on my first trek to Surrey but on the next one, I was lucky enough to find that the address for my mother's husband had turned out to be a boarding house. The elderly lady still resided there, and she said she remembered him/them, and told me that to the best of her knowledge they had moved to the next town along the way, so to speak.

There was absolutely no way of knowing, of course, whether they had remained in that area—after all it was thirty-five or so years ago—but I was nothing if not optimistic.

I purchased and then scanned the telephone directories for the area; their name was quite a common one, and so there were dozens but the ones with the initial A only took up half a page or so.

Had they moved on anyway, as was highly likely, I was on a wild goose chase.

I had no plan of action...I hadn't rehearsed what I was going to say and in my heart of hearts I don't think I really thought I would find her.

Nothing in my life had been that easy, so why should this be any different?

The gods must really have been with me. After a few phone calls which had got me nowhere, I connected to a gentleman who confirmed that he was indeed the named person I was seeking.

With a tremor in my voice I asked if his wife was called Sheila. Not surprisingly, he queried why I wanted to know and considering that my knees were knocking together in sheer terror and I was clinging on to my bed (I had decided that the best place to carry out this manoeuvre was in the relative peace of my bedroom away from the hustle and bustle of kids, dogs and chaos), I managed to answer in a reasonably articulate way, despite being totally unrehearsed, and said I was trying to organise a reunion with my friends in the Forces. Amazingly, he seemed to find this plausible and said, yes indeed, his wife was Sheila and, hold on, he'd just call her.

In what was probably no more than a couple of seconds but seemed like an eternity to me for I had no idea whatsoever what I was going to say (the social worker's warning sprung to mind: natural parents may well in their current lifestyle have partners and families totally unaware of their past history, so tread very carefully), I was saved from what felt, in the heat of that moment, a fate worse than death, by his returning to say his wife was in the bath, could I call later…?

With utter relief, I muttered something unintelligible and hung up.

I sat, lost in my own little world for probably nigh on an hour before going downstairs and announcing to my unsuspecting family, 'I've found my mum.' Then the sheer emotion of the moment enveloped me and I convulsed, sobbing, into the warmth of their embraces.

Knowing where to reach her, and actually doing so were

two different things and it was several weeks before I plucked up the courage to dial that number again.

It wasn't that I didn't want to—I had probably never wanted anything so badly in my life, and my fingers ached to pick up that phone. Thinking about it occupied my every waking moment, but I was so scared.

There were so many what-ifs…pre-conceived ideas about what you can or can't take in the way of negative responses don't mean a thing when it comes to the real moment. I had to build up an overwhelming bank of courage to cope with the possibility of rejection.

I rehearsed over and over what I would say.

I had decided that I would ring in the daytime when it was likely her husband would be at work and she would be the one to answer the phone. I had toyed with writing a letter, just a brief note asking her to ring this number…but what if she didn't respond?—No, it had to be the phone.

At least I would hear her voice, even if it were to be for the first and last time.

I rang…but no response. The phone rang and rang, and the disappointment I felt was indescribable. The wait for a couple of hours to go by before trying again was interminable.

This time, it was picked up on the second ring, a light, friendly voice, not dissimilar to mine. 'Is that Sheila?' Affirmative.

'Well I think I have some news, which might be rather a shock to you…I think I may be your daughter…'

This time the silence was not imagined; it must have been for all of three or four minutes and what was going on in her mind I can only guess at—you could have heard a pin drop. Then back came the rejoinder: 'Oh, how clever of you to find me.'

We chatted on the phone in that first instance for probably half an hour, thirty-odd years of my life condensed into as many minutes, it's crazy isn't it?

What did transpire was that her husband was not aware of a daughter from her past, and so I have to confess to momentary disappointment that he, her spouse, was not indeed as I had dared to let myself hope, my father.

That first conversation remains only a dim recollection. We had several others in closer proximity in which we both tentatively explored the lifetime gap of knowing nothing about each other, but for those first precious moments it was enough to know that here was the very being that had given me the most precious gift of all, life—my mum.

I had been born at the end of the war, a fling I guess. My father was Jewish, fun-loving, youngest son of a family with a clothing factory in the East End (what Jewish family didn't in those days!), keen to have a good time and Sheila, following a broken romance, was a willing consort. Her family were the epitome of middle-class urban respectability—staunch C of E, you get the picture I am sure. They were worlds apart in culture and background, their friendship not meeting with approval from either family. I gathered it wasn't the romance of the century, just a good time, so I don't suppose it mattered much to either of them.

When she had found she was pregnant, in the height of the panic, she had felt that they ought to get married but, quite rightly, he'd said that it would be for all the wrong reasons and maintained that he would support me but not marry on such shaky foundations.

Sheila was an only child, ironically like me, adopted. This was why I couldn't find her birth certificate when I had searched, as it would have been in the Adopted Children's Registers.

Whilst she was not particularly forthcoming about her own lifestyle as a child, it transpired she had not had the happiest childhood in the world though. Set firmly in the middle-class cloistered environment of which she was a part, the knowledge that she was pregnant went down like a lead balloon, and it was out of the question that she should be seen to have an illegitimate baby, let alone keep it!!

And so she was despatched to a Mother and Baby home, which is where Brockett Hall came in, hidden away until after my birth. When everything was done and dusted, neatly tucked under the carpet, she was able to return home again as if the whole incident had never happened, no one any the wiser.

I listened to her story as it unfolded; it must have been similar to a great many others relating to post-war babies.

I think I made the appropriate responses, outwardly concurring with everything she was telling me, yes; it had in all probability been for the best.

Inwardly I was screaming, 'Well why didn't you stand up for yourself and say you wanted to keep me?' But this was only wishful thinking on my part. In reality, she probably didn't want me, and was quite happy to go with the flow, the easy option, comply with her mother's wishes; after all, that was what happened, wasn't it?

Not particularly forthcoming about my father either, although she seemed to speak with fondness of him, she said she had kept briefly in touch with him, but that he had been ill and died of leukaemia when I was eighteen months old and the rest was history.

She married eighteen months later and had remained very happily so ever since. Her partner was completely unaware of past history. It happened!

Very sadly for her, she had not been successful in raising a family. They had decided to establish careers and make other priorities and waited for almost ten years before trying to start a family. They had, after their marriage, moved to London, so how lucky I was that they had returned to their roots (fate rearing its head again)! She had lost two little boys, one stillborn the other just a few days old.

Following the birth of her third son, who had also experienced a few difficulties, she had called a halt. My half-brother is just a couple of years older than my daughter Dawn.

Now here she is, through a sudden twist of fate, discovering not only a daughter, but three lovely grandchildren too. I hope she felt it an enriching experience.

How did I feel?

I wish she had been a better liar…I wanted her to tell me that she had missed me every day, thought of me constantly, and regretted giving me away. But she didn't.

Like many others probably in similar situations, she had just got on with her life. Certainly she had thought of me on occasions, like my birthday, but I didn't occupy her every waking moment.

I wanted to have done! I wanted her to tell me she was bereft. I realise it was illogical. Truth hurts, I guess.

As I got to know her better, I realised that she was really quite self-sufficient, had enjoyed a rich and fulfilling lifestyle and that there was no way she was going to clasp me to her bosom saying, 'My darling, my life has been empty without you,'—you know the sort of thing, the stuff dreams are made of...

At least she didn't actually tell me she led too busy a lifestyle to fit me in and I'm sure she was too kind to have ever done so, but that reaction did come from her husband the first time we met, all those years ago. He said that Sheila led a very busy and full life and didn't have time to fit anything else in, that they already had family on his side that occupied their time, and so on.

Good thoroughly demoralising stuff!

But at least he had the integrity to respond truthfully when I asked him whether, if what he said was the case, had Sheila not been pleased that I had got in touch with her?

There followed a short silence after which he said, 'No, I couldn't say that, she was over the moon!' Thank you, Arthur, for giving me that little bit of self-esteem. I suspect it was just his defence mechanism working; it must have been such an almighty shock to have your world, as you know it, turned upside down.

But I am digressing; came the point when, after a few phone calls and letters (her family at that time were still not aware of my existence), we decided to meet for the first time.

I chose a hotel in London that I was familiar with, having used it in connection with my work. Yes, it was a very posh one; subconsciously perhaps I was seeking reassurance for my insecurity, this tumultuous hurdle, trying to impress, who knows?

On that morning, preparing for the meeting, my partner had to dress me like a baby; my hands were perspiring so much I couldn't fasten the cuffs of my Laura Ashley blouse. I had chosen a black corduroy overdress and, just to complete the ensemble, my arctic fox jacket—every inch the successful young businesswomen.

Distinctly overdressed!

Probably overdressing for just the same reasons as I had chosen one of the better hotels, I guess—my security blanket, to show that I had made something of my life perhaps…again, who knows…?

I wasn't a materialistic person—expensive furs were not remotely important to me; this one had been a gift and I never did like the damn thing. By the time I got up to Euston on the train, it had moulted so much that my black dress looked like a cat with mange!

I collapsed in the toilets sobbing my heart out, my self-confidence in tatters.

Fortunately an extremely kind lavatory attendant took pity on me and a roll of cellotape later (which she popped into the stationers to buy), chastened, I was on my way again, only this time the wretched thing was turned inside out over my arm. I was very tempted to dump it in the litterbin!

They might have been the 'in' thing to have in those days but it was a bright day for me when having animal furs was deemed politically incorrect and I could legitimately dispose of it in the dustbin without my conscience nagging for all of the money it had cost.

Arriving at the hotel, my heart was pounding, pulses racing. I had been on a few blind dates in my time, but nothing like this!

In the busy foyer of the hotel, I sank into the luxurious folds of a deeply upholstered settee and watched the hustle and bustle of people going about their busy lives.

I had this imagined picture of my mother: she would be extremely well groomed, immaculately coiffured, probably wearing a designer outfit that would have cost me a month of hard work in my employment agency to earn the money to pay for.

I don't know where I had drawn this preconceived idea from (perhaps associated with my Brockett Hall, blue-blooded conception). Well, I had to be special, didn't I?

There were many ladies who fitted this bill: I scanned them all, but none seemed to recognise or to be looking for little old me. (I had sent her a photograph, but the one she had sent to me had been taken many years previously.)

No one was taking the slightest notice of me.

There was a lady standing near the reception desks; she was wearing a light summery suit and seemed to have a clipboard in her arms, just a very ordinary, normal person. So I dismissed her after a cursory glance, thinking perhaps she was doing some market research.

After probably an hour, the foyer thinned out, and the lady by the desk and I were two of the few remaining. Tentatively she made her way across to me: 'Are you by any chance Sandie?'

Quick to comment on the age of the photograph I had of her, equally the photograph she clutched of me showed a dark-haired lass, before my love affair with the bleach bottle...and thus she had dismissed this fair young lady, seeking one with dark sultry locks.

We laughed over the misconception and somehow this broke the ice and together we left to, on my part anyway, feast on each other as well as the delicious lunch, which the White House was renowned for. If you were to ask me what we had eaten, I wouldn't have had a clue, it could have been cardboard, so eager was I to cram into that extended lunchtime a lifetime of catching up.

I'm sure she felt the same way.

And thus I met my mum.

I'd like to say we lived happily ever after and she fulfilled everything I was seeking in my life, but this is the real world.

Ironically, the questions I had about my origins remained unanswered, as my biological or true father was dead, and my mother knew nothing at all about her own background, having been adopted. (Her adopted parents were both deceased.) She clearly had no wish to look into her own pre-adoption background which of course, I had to respect, so it was a stalemate situation really.

As fond as she is of me and I of her, too many years of my not being a part of her life, of not having that very special mother-daughter relationship, were just too wide a gap to bridge, and we have never really bonded into the partnership of mother and daughter. Friends, yes.

I wanted it to happen, but it just wasn't there. My mother, in her own way, cares about me, my children and indeed her great grandchildren, but not in that extra special way that I have to confess, in spite of my brave assertion that I could accept anything, I was really hoping for.

I wanted it so much in those early days, but reconciled myself to the fact that it just wasn't going to happen as the years passed by.

I love my children more than life itself, so in my naïveté it seemed inconceivable that she shouldn't feel the same way. She certainly didn't; I don't judge her for that, in any way.

Her son, who sadly does have difficulties, has never wanted me or my family to overlap into his life or, if the truth be known, to share his parents. Of course that is entirely his choice, which in turn, I fully respect and understand. After all, we're all human. As an only child, he has nothing in his life other than his parents whereas I am so very lucky in the love and warmth of my family whom I adore, so I have nothing to grumble about.

Although Sheila and I do not have that 'magical' ingredient, we do care for each other and I have come to terms with the relationship for what it is.

Life is too short to let it get to me; I count my blessings that we met, that she has had the opportunity to know her daughter and grandchildren, and her life has been enriched a little for that as ours has for knowing her. But there is a tiny little part of me buried in the very deepest regions of my heart, that cries out that I would have liked to have been someone's very special little girl again.

*C'est la vie.*

Louise did show me that extra special bond of love in the short time she had with me and nothing will ever eclipse that. She will always be my mum, and occupy that special place in my heart. Sheila is a special person too, for she gave me the gift of life and some of the genes with which to make a success of it.

Thank you, Sheila.

Friday's child has come a full circle.

# REFLECTION

I'm looking at a chocolate cupcake with a solitary candle lit, and stuck awkwardly in the middle, three tear-stained faces looking soulfully up at me. They are devastated because the enormously expensive chocolate cake they had clubbed together to buy from a patisserie in a fashionable resort in the South of France, utilising almost all of their holiday spending money (on what was the first holiday we had managed to scrape the money up for in many years), had been stolen from the camp site office where they had stored it for 'safe' keeping. Homemade cards and gifts of great ingenuity and thought are being proffered with so much love for their mum.

It is my thirtieth birthday; the gift of love and belonging they bestow on me is priceless.

The lump in my throat threatens to take over my entire body as I hug them, never wanting to let them go, feasting on the joy that they bring to me, fulfilling, enriching my life. If I spare a thought for that soulful child of more than a decade ago now, facing her thirteenth birthday at the hands of her tormentors, it is with quiet confidence, knowing that I have overcome, that my experiences of life have made me a stronger, worthier person, empowering me to be a better human being.

Happy Birthday, Friday's Child.

# Author's Notes

It has taken me fifty years to write *Friday's Child*, to have the courage to bring to the surface memories hitherto deeply buried in the innermost sanctuary of my mind. Ultimately it is a story of hope, of searching to find myself, overcoming those obstacles that threatened to consume me.

What spurred me on was David Pelzer's book, *A Child Called It*...how my heart went out to him, his sheer determination to survive against all the odds. I felt, illogically perhaps, that my experiences faded into insignificance in comparison and yet the book set me to wondering just how many of us are out there?

Now we are hit with statistics that one in four children now suffer abuse, I am saddened by the world we live in and, yet, what of my generation? How many of us were 'victims' without the benefits of the many agencies who have the protection of these vulnerable children at heart today? The 1989 Children's Act sought to tighten the net and to offer children the right to protection and we justly strive very hard to give it but there will always be those children who slip through it—those we read about in stark horror and unfortunately all too many that we don't ever know about. There always has been and always will be children out there who struggle with their tormentors and whose (often silent) cries for help go unnoticed.

Why silent? Because so many abused children, myself included, are convinced that it is something 'we' have done wrong and all too often we have this inexplicable loyalty towards our tormenters or, to put it another way, we love them. We go back time and time again with forgiveness in our hearts and the unspoken plea:

Let this be the day you love me...

All I have ever wanted in my life is to be loved, to give love. The scars run deep, in spite of the confident façade I give out; I still cannot cope with rejection and I doubt that I will ever truly overcome this insecurity.

I have often been asked how I felt about my father? Truthfully, in spite of everything that he was responsible for, the hurt, the rejection, the condoning of what was happening to me, he was, and always will be in my thoughts, 'my dad'. Throughout my life, adolescence, transition into a mature woman, during the reconciliation we had in the twilight years of his life I never stopped trying to be back in that special place in his heart. Illogical, irrational? That's life I guess, we are complex beings, aren't we?

I realise now of course that Alice had featured in his life whilst my mother was still alive, and so very ill, which explains the friction and severance of ties with my mother's family after her death. At the time it affected me greatly, but I don't hold that against him. Louise, my mum, was acutely ill; understandably this had put some strains on the relationship. For many years they led a patient and carer lifestyle instead of that of husband and wife. I know absolutely though that she was and always was, the love of his life.

In writing my story and sharing my experiences, it has made me realise that it wasn't my fault! It wasn't in any way deserved and I was just the victim of circumstances, of other people's instability and insecurity.

That doesn't condone what I suffered and I can never forgive the way my happy childhood was so abruptly cut short to be replaced with anguish and yes, terror, but I can now rationalise *why*. For me, knowing so much love in those early years made it somehow so much harder to accept what so suddenly became 'my lot'.

Alice had never had a happy childhood; an only child, she was illegitimate and although her own mother—the 'wicked witch'—had married a kindly man who had loved her as his own, and whom Alice had adored, he had died prematurely. Her mother had never got over the stigma of having a child out of wedlock (as indeed it was in the 'twenties), and had vented her frustration and anger on Alice throughout her life.

Abused, as she herself was, her role as abuser was only directed at me and not at her own children.

Alice was a victim of mental illness through much of her life. Because of her introverted lifestyle it remained undiagnosed and thus untreated, or she could have received a great deal more in the way of help and support and I might not have needed to write this book.

Alice died suddenly in the 1980s, when in her fifties, of a heart attack. We were never reconciled in any way.

I have always been a great believer in fate, in destiny, my karma, and over the years I have seen some excellent clairvoyants and mediums. On two occasions when I have consulted mediums at opposite sides of the country, Alice has been present, both times giving her name.

In the first reading she didn't speak, just proffered flowers but in the second, quite a few years later, Alice passed on a message that she was truly sorry. She indicated she had been extremely jealous of me, not—as I had always assumed—of my relationship with my father, but of my confidence and zest for living: something she had never had as a child or as an adult.

'Sorry'—that word means so much and is so hard to say. I write in my book about the joys brought to me by discovering a new family in my husband's brother and sister-in-law and their family. It was wonderful for me, only to be abruptly brought to an end for no reason. My brother-in-law was possibly in a relationship somewhere, maybe using me as an excuse—perhaps, I have no idea really. All I know is that it most certainly wasn't me! At his funeral many years later, his widow told my daughter who attended with her father (she incidentally had no recollection of having met him), 'I once did your mother a very great injustice for which I am truly sorry.' She knew she was wrong, I doubt that she knew the heartache this closing door would inflict on me but she never once attempted to contact me to put the matter to rights.

My father, now in spirit, (he died in his eighties) did try to make amends and we enjoyed a closer fulfilling relationship again in his twilight years. I forgive him.

From the spirit world via a medium, about my book he said, 'You don't pull any punches, girl, but you tell it like it is.'

I hope I have.

END